WHO SHOT JFK?

A Guide to the Major Conspiracy Theories

Bob Callahan

Illustrated By
Mark Zingarelli

A FIRESIDE BOOK
Published by Simon & Schuster
New York   London   Toronto   Sydney   Tokyo   Singapore

Acknowledgments

The author would like to extend grateful acknowledgments to Warren Hinckle, Paul Hoch, Josiah Thompson, and Peter Dale Scott, whose own contributions to this case are reviewed in these pages; to friends Art Spiegelman and T. J. English, who listened patiently as I often discussed this project into the wee hours of the night; and to my son David, now a freshman at the University of Massachusetts in Boston, who ably reminded me when it was time to give it a break.

Finally, on behalf of the entire staff, I should like to pay particular thanks to our editor, Sheridan Hay, whose guidance and support made this book possible. *Who Shot JFK?* is dedicated to Robert Ranftel, who died just before this project began. Bob gave some of his best years to working on this puzzle, and his intelligence and good cheer remains an inspiration to all of us lucky enough to have been his friends.

Author: Bob Callahan
Illustrator: Mark Zingarelli
Art Director/Design: E. J. Muller
Editor: Sheridan Hay
Project Editors: Bob Callahan, E. J. Muller
Research Associates: David Park, John Kelly
Copy Editor: Erik S. McMahon
Production: Jacqueline Hughes-Killen
Representation: Norman Kurz, Barbara Lowenstein

FIRESIDE BOOKS
Simon & Schuster Building
Rockefeller Center
1230 Avenue of the Americas
New York, New York 10020
FIRESIDE and colophon are registered trademarks of Simon & Schuster
Manufactured in the United States of America
10 9 8 7 6 5 4 3 2 1
Library of Congress Cataloging-in-Publication Data
Callahan, Bob.
Who shot JFK?: a guide to the major conspiracy theories / Bob Callahan; illustrated by Mark Zingarelli.
p. cm. —(A Fireside book)
Includes bibliographical references and index.
1. Kennedy, John F. (John Fitzgerald), 1917-1963—Assassination.
I. Zingarelli, Mark. II. Title.
E842.9.C355 1993
364.1'524—dc20   93-8415
CIP
ISBN: 0-671-79494-9

TABLE OF CONTENTS

BOOK ONE
MURDER ON ELM STREET

BOOK TWO
THE FALL OF THE HOUSE OF WARREN

BOOK FOUR

A QUESTION OF TREASON

F ew of us look at politics and politicians the way we did before John Kennedy was assassinated. The fear, anger, and pain unleashed in Dealey Plaza succeeded in turning a generation of idealistic children into a generation of political outlaws and social misfits. After JFK's murder, and Bobby's, and Watergate, Vietnam, and Dr. King; Malcolm X, the S&Ls, and Iran-Contra, too—it's still impossible to see how one might ever truly fit into an order of political succession based on murder, deception and crime. To a great extent, misfits we still remain.

In the years which have passed since the death of JFK, a strange new genre of literature—postmodern at base, wildly apocalyptic in its assertions—has grown up in this country like so many weeds in the garden, like so many rabbit holes on the prairie plains. For thirty years now, this literature has attempted to provide a measure for our loss, and for our pain.

Who Shot JFK? is the first book to seriously concentrate on the literature of John Kennedy's assassination. The book has been created for concerned people who don't have the time to read for themselves all the major books, pamphlets and government reports directly connected with this ongoing investigation. Presented in a digest format, with particular attention to how the various controversies have emerged over time, *Who Shot JFK?* offers the reader a comprehensive review of the major theories, incidents, and compelling suspects associated with modern America's most profoundly political murder mystery.

Each new and serious theory is treated with the attention it deserves. As for the more preposterous materials which have also worked their way into the text, I can only hope the reader will forgive the gallows humor which is offered to relieve the weight of what can become at times a truly bizarre, and hideous murder case. The serious material is treated seriously. As for the rest, well, it's not like we have anything in principle against the notion that the real JFK is still alive, and living on a factory farm outside Minsk. It just doesn't seem all that likely.

Who Shot JFK? attempts to honor equally all of the intelligent and thoughtful theories concerning the death of John Kennedy. Although the reader will have no difficulty locating our own opinion in this matter, this book does not attempt to force any single point of view upon its readers. We have used such intelligence as we have—along with an abiding interest in the new graphic literature—to provide what is hopefully an open-minded, casebook guide to the assassination of JFK. The most profound, yet hardly original, conclusion we have reached is that John Kennedy's real killers have not yet been fully identified. We think they should be. Seldom in history have such men been able to so boldly rob an entire nation of the legitimacy of their own political system, and the ability to dream. Who killed JFK? The case is still open. And it has been raining now, steadily, for more than thirty years.

—**Bob Callahan**

The literature concerning the assassination of John Fitzgerald Kennedy begins with the transcript of Dallas District Attorney Henry Wade's press conference from November 24, 1963. Reading the transcript the next morning in the *New York Times*, attorney Mark Lane made notes which would quickly lead to the first published article critical of the official story of the killing.

From such basic techno-legal beginnings a vast and fascinating political literature would grow. More than 2,500 books, and at least twice that many monographs and articles, would be published about JFK's murder over the next thirty years.

Four European writers—Thomas Buchanan, Hans Habe, Joachim Joesten, and Leo Sauvage— would soon follow Lane's initiative, and join the Conspiracy Choir. Not to be outdone, certain American left and right wing groups would also enter the game.

By the spring of 1964, a related story dominated the public's consciousness: the trial of Jack Ruby. Of all the various early Ruby writings, Murray Kempton's offerings in both the American and English press have best stood up to the test of time.

Then, in September, the Warren Commission stepped forward to release its much awaited Official Report. The report managed to momentarily quiet the critics, and it brought this early era of JKF assassination literature to an uneasy close.

The Prosecution Makes Its Case

The Henry Wade Press Conference Controversy

O n Sunday evening, November 24, 1963—just two days after the President had been killed, and only hours after the President's alleged assailant had himself been murdered while in the custody of Dallas Police—Dallas District Attorney Henry Wade convened the world press to talk about his case against Lee Harvey Oswald. Wade very much wanted the world to know that in spite of the chaos, the city of Dallas was still in charge.

At the time Wade enjoyed a considerable reputation in Dallas judicial circles. Since his appointment to his position in 1950, he had sought the death penalty in 24 different cases. Twenty-three times the court had agreed with him.

A member of one of Texas's most prominent legal families—his father was a Rockwell County judge; seven of his brothers had become either judges or lawyers—Wade had also spent time as an undercover agent for the FBI during the Second World War. He had been active in New York harbor, at the time the US Navy had sought the help of mobster Lucky Luciano to counter potential Axis sabotage attempts. He had also worked for a time doing anti-Nazi undercover work in Colombia. The city of Dallas would thus be served by a seasoned professional.

"THE PURPOSE OF THIS news conference," Wade began, "is to detail some of the evidence against Oswald for the assassination of the President."

Wade turned first to the so-called sniper's nest. "First there was a number of witnesses that saw the person with the gun on the sixth floor of the bookstore building, the window—detailing the window—where he was looking out. Inside this window the police found a row of bookcases, boxes, hiding someone, sitting in the window, from people on the same floor... On this box the defendant was sitting on, his palm print was found, and was identified as his."

The District Attorney then turned his attention to the rifle. "Three ejected shells were found right by the box. The gun was hidden on this same floor behind some bookcases and boxes. It has been identified as having been purchased last March by Oswald, from a mail-order house, through an assumed name named Hidell, mailed to a post office box here in Dallas. On his person was a pocketbook. In his pocketbook was an identification card with the same name as the post office box on it. Pictures were [also] found of the defendant with his gun and a pistol on his—in his—holster."

W̲ADE WENT ON TO LOCATE BOTH OSWALD, AND his rifle, inside the Texas School Book Depository at the time of the shooting. "[Oswald] carried [to work with him that morning] a package under his arm that he said was window curtains, I believe, or window shades. The wife said he had the gun the night before and it was missing that morning after he left. A police officer, immediately after the assassination, ran in the building and saw this man in a corner, and tried to arrest him, but the manager of the building said he was an employee and it was all right. Every other employee was [later] located but this defendant."

Wade sketched out Oswald's further crimes. "The next we hear of him is on a bus on Lamar Street. He told the bus driver the President had been shot. 'Yes, he's been shot," [Oswald] said, and laughed very loud. He [then] got off the bus at a stop, caught a taxicab driver, Darryl Click, and went to his home in Oak Cliff, changed his clothes hurriedly, and left.

"A block or two from his house," Wade continued, "three witnesses saw as police officer J.D. Tippit motioned to him, or said something to him. He walked up to the car. Officer Tippit stepped out of the car and started around it. He [Oswald] shot him three times and killed him."

Wade concluded with the arrest. "[Oswald] walked across a vacant lot. Witnesses saw him eject the shells

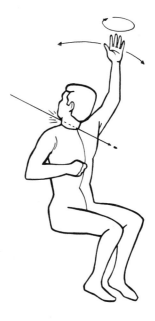

The Life Magazine Theory

According to Paul Mandel's report in the December 6, 1963 issue of LIFE, a Parkland doctor who had tried to save the President reported that one of the bullets entered the President's throat and then lodged in his body. "Since by this time the limousine was 50 yards past Oswald and the President's back was turned almost directly to the sniper, it has been hard to understand how the bullet could enter the front of his throat. Hence the recurring guess that there was a second sniper somewhere else. But the 8mm film shows the President turning his body far around to the right as he waves to someone in the crowd. His throat is exposed— toward the sniper's nest— just before he clutches it."

from a revolver and reload the gun. Someone saw him go in the Texas Theater. A search was made. An officer of the Dallas police spotted him and asked him to come out. He struck at the officer, put the gun against his [the officer's] head, and snapped it, but did not—the bullet did not— go off."

"His fingerprints were found on this gun," Wade added, almost as an afterthought. "Parrafin tests also show that he had recently fired a gun—it was on both hands."

THE DISTRICT ATTORNEY then took a few questions from the press. "Did he ever admit anything at all?" Wade was asked.

"He never did admit any of the killing," the DA responded.

"Did he display any animosity toward the President?"

"He was bitter toward all of the officers that examined him is what I've been told," said Wade.

"Do you know that he has been recognized as a patron of Ruby's nightclub here," one of the reporters inquired.

"I don't know that," Wade flatly concluded.

Oswald was the man who had killed President Kennedy, of that Wade was certain. "I have sent men to the electric chair with less evidence," the Dallas District Attorney would later say.

An Early End to Nagging Rumors

The Dallas D.A. may have been satisfied that he had his man, but the rest of the country certainly wanted more information before it would be able to put its collective imagination to rest. In the December 6, 1963 issue of *Life* , reporter Paul Mandel addressed the case's fundamental questions in a simple question and answer format.

"Was it really Oswald who shot the President," *Life* asked?

"Yes," the magazine declared. "The evidence against him is circumstantial and it received an incredibly bush-league battering around by the Dallas police, but it appears to be positive."

How many shots were fired? Three, *Life* stated. Where were the shots fired from? Lee Harvey Oswald's place of employment—The Texas School Book Depository.

But here *Life* ran into a problem which would keep this controversy alive for the next three decades. "Many rumors have grown out of the presumed difficulty of firing three accurate shots in the time Oswald had," the magazine noted, "and at the ranges over which he fired. But an 8mm film of the assassination provides a frame-by-frame chronology of events, and from the movie camera's known speed of 18 frames a second it is possible to reconstruct the precise timing and placing and feasibility of the shots.

"The first strikes the President in the throat; 74 frames later, the second fells Governor Connally; 48 frames after that, the third, over a distance of 260 feet, hits the President's head. From first to second shot 4.1 seconds elapse; from second to third, 2.7 seconds. Altogether, the three shots take 6.8 seconds—time enough for a trained sharpshooter, even through the bobbing field of a telescopic sight... Oswald was an ex-Marine sharpshooter, and he was firing from a perfect sniper's position."

The film that allowed *Life*—and later the Warren Commission—to clock the shots was the now famous Zapruder home movie which *Life* had purchased from Dallas dress manufacturer, and amateur photographer, Abraham Zapruder.

The Zapruder film would not, however, be shown to the American public in its entirety until 1975. As government officials even then were aware, *Life* had in fact made a mistake in this account of the firing. First of all, Oswald was hardly a sharpshooter. Marine records showed that he was less than even an average shot on the firing range. Even more importantly, a close viewing of the Zapruder film shows that Governor Connally is hit a mere 1.8 seconds after the President is first wounded.

One point eight seconds; and yet, as the FBI already knew at the time of *Life*'s December report, it would take 2.3 seconds to reload and fire the alleged murder rifle.

In Defense of Lee Harvey Oswald

The First Mark Lane Controversy

The morning after District Attorney Henry Wade's press conference, Brooklyn attorney Mark Lane read a transcript of that conference in the November 26, 1963 issue of the *New York Times*. "When I sat down to analyze the charges to place them alongside what was then known about the case, I quickly found that the weaknesses were blatant," Lane would later say. He transformed his notes into a 10,000 word article, which, he soon learned, no one on his list of New York publishing contacts wanted to touch with a ten-foot pole. Editors at *Look*, *LIFE*, *The Saturday Evening Post*, the *New York Post*, the *New Republic* and even *The Progressive* all took a pass before the Marxist *National Guardian* agreed to publish the piece in its December 19, 1963 issue.

"In all likelihood," Lane began, "there does not exist a single American community where reside 12 men or women, good and true, who presume that Lee Harvey Oswald did not assassinate President Kennedy. The reader, inundated at the outset with 48 solid television, radio and newspaper hours devoted to proving the guilt of the accused...cannot now examine this case without bringing to it certain preconceived ideas. [As difficult as this may be to provide] we ask, instead, only for a temporary suspension of certainty."

In the manner of a defense lawyer presenting his brief, Lane challenged the fifteen assertions of guilt which formed the basis of Dallas D.A. Henry Wade's case against Oswald.

WADE ASSERTED THAT A NUMBER OF WITnesses had seen Oswald at the sixth floor window of the book depository. *Lane countered that only one witness had made such a claim, and that this witness later told* Newsweek *he would be unable to identify Oswald if he saw him.*

•

Oswald's palmprint was found on the rifle. *Lane countered that Oswald's palmprint was not found on the rifle.*

•

Oswald's palmprint was also found on one of the cardboard boxes which made up the sniper's nest. *Lane countered that this box had been removed from the sixth floor of the Book Depository, and that Oswald could have left a palmprint on the box while under interrogation at the Dallas Police Department.*

•

Parrafin tests showed that Oswald had recently fired a gun—"it was on both of his hands," Wade said. *Lane countered that the tests were inconclusive on this point.*

•

The rifle found on the sixth floor of the School Book Depository was an Italian Mannlicher-Carcano. *The rifle was first identified as a German Mauser, Lane countered.*

•

An identification card made out for "A. Hidell" had been "discovered" on Oswald's person. *Lane wondered why this was a separate assertion, as Dallas officials had already determined that Oswald had bought his rifle by mail-order under the false name of "A. Hidell."*

•

Oswald had been stopped, and almost arrested, by a Dallas police officer who had rushed into the building immediately after the assassination. *Lane noted that Oswald, when confronted by police, was in the second floor lunchroom, quietly sipping a coke, and not on the sixth floor where the shots were allegedly fired.*

•

Wade asserted that Marina Oswald had noted that Oswald's rifle was missing from its storage space on the morning of the shooting. *Lane maintained that Marina had not made such a statement.*

•

Oswald had carried his rifle into work with him that morning in a package which he had told a fellow worker contained window curtain rods or window shades. *There was no evidence to suggest that package contained a rifle. Lane argued.*

•

Oswald had caused an uproar on a public bus in the hour after the assassination, laughing loudly about JFK's murder. *The FBI had already admitted that this incident was entirely fictitious, Lane countered.*

•

Oswald had gotten off the bus after this incident, and was driven to his apartment by cab driver Darryl Click . *The cab driver was not Click, but William Whaley, and his cab log showed that he picked up Oswald a few minutes before the President was shot and killed.*

•

The Coca-Cola Theory

The news that Oswald had been sipping a Coca-Cola in the second floor lunchroom of the Texas School Book Depository struck a responsive chord in the mind of the one of the most unusual of all assassination critics. According to Edward Epstein, this fact led health crusader J. I. Rodale, the editor of *Organic Gardening and Farming*, to surmise "Oswald was not responsible for his action: his brain was confused because he was a sugar drunkard. What is called for now is a full-scale investigation of sugar consumption and crime."

Wade had seemed confused as to where Oswald allegedly shot and killed Officer Tippit; he had listed three separate locations. *Lane challenged that confusion, asking why the D.A. hadn't been more specific.*

•

Wade asserted that the cashier at the Texas Theater had first called the police because Oswald acted in a suspicious manner. *Lane wondered what was so suspicious about a customer attending a matinee movie.*

•

Oswald had attempted to shoot the arresting officer, and he had the gun, and the bullet where the faulty firing pin had struck it, in his possession. *No such bullet existed, Lane claimed, as the arresting officer had taken the gun away from Oswald before he had the chance to pull the trigger.*

•

After his press conference, Wade had added a fifteenth assertion—that the Dallas Police had found in Oswald's possession a map of the key assassination sites. *Lane wondered why the map wasn't introduced earlier, at the press conference, as it seemed to be a very important piece of evidence indeed.*

WHAT LANE CREATED WAS A BRIEF FOR THE Defense. And that was terribly important. Ten months later the Warren Commission would respond with a brief for the Prosecution.

The search for the truth of Dealey Plaza would be clouded from the first by the ambition and mannerisms of adversarial lawyers. Lane, however, had made his point. In legal terms, Lee Harvey Oswald could hardly be considered guilty beyond a reasonable doubt.

With courtroom justice as its chosen form, the debate was now open, and before long it seemed like almost everyone had their own opinion on what really happened that sad day in Dallas, thirty years ago.

His Mother's Son
A MANCHURIAN CANDIDATE FOR DEALEY PLAZA

ON DECEMBER 28, 1963, NOVELIST RICHARD CONDON WROTE an article in *The Nation* entitled "Manchurian Candidate in Dallas." Condon was the author of *The Manchurian Candidate*, which had been made into a popular motion picture.

The film concerned an American officer brainwashed by the Red Chinese during the Korean War, who returns to America programmed to kill the President. Condon found striking similarities between his fictional candidate, Raymond Shaw, and Lee Harvey Oswald.

"Oswald's wife said she married him because she felt sorry for him; absolutely no one had liked him, 'even in Russia.'," Condon writes."[My] novel says: "It was not that Raymond was hard to like. He was impossible to like."

"Oswald spoke frequently of the hardships his mother experienced in the depression, before he had been born, and his mother had been quick to say that *they* had always been against her boy. In the novel, I quoted Andrew Salter, the Pavlovian psychologist: ...'the human fish swim about at the bottom of the great ocean of atmosphere and they develop psychic injuries as they collide with one another. Most mortal to these are the wounds gotten from the parent fish.'"

"The Associated Press dug up a truancy report on Oswald which said his resentment had been fixed on 'authority.' On the surface he was calm, but inside there was much anger. 'The resenters,' says the Chinese brainwasher in *The Manchurian Candidate*, "those men with cancer of the psyche, make the great assassins."

FOR CONDON, PARALLELS BETWEEN SHAW AND OSWALD break apart in the end. Shaw was programmed by Chinese intelligence; Oswald, according to Condon, was influenced by his resentment of the charming and successful Kennedy, and by the excessive violence inherent in our culture.

Fifteen years later, Condon's early remarks would take on a darker edge when it was learned that, in attempting to create the perfect political assassin, the CIA—like Condon's Red Chinese—had been in the mind control business from 1954, through the period of the Kennedy assassination. Indeed, on the very day of Kennedy's death, an officer in the CIA was meeting with an agent—code name, AM/LASH— who was about to be sent back into Havana to assassinate Fidel Castro. The meeting was terminated when the news from Dallas reached The Company.

It Could Never Happen Here

The Buchanan "Who Killed Kennedy" Controversy

In the days, weeks and months immediately following the murder of John Fitzgerald Kennedy, journalists on both sides of the Atlantic began to debate the history of American political assassinations. The theme was first sounded by reporter Foster Hailey, in a piece entitled "Lone Assassin the Rule in U.S.; Plotting More Prevalent Abroad," which appeared in the November 26, 1963 edition of the *New York Times.*

"A study of assassination attempts of the last century in the three countries where they have been most frequent—Czarist Russia, Japan, and the United States," Hailey began, "reveals no clear pattern or motivation beyond a common urge to right a wrong. There is one clear distinction [however] between most of the attempts to kill Government figures in other countries and those in the United States.

"In Russia and in Japan the assassinations generally were the culmina-

tion of the detailed plans made by well-organized groups, usually involving high Government figures. The motivations were political, or nationalistic.

"In the United States, in all except two cases, the attempts were made by a single person often with advance planning, and often without any real grievance against the personage attacked. That seems to have been the case with Lee Harvey Oswald, the killer of President Kennedy.

Three days later, *Time* took the point even further. "Assassination has never been an instrument of politics in the U.S.A.," the magazine declared. "No plot to seize power, no palace intrigue, has ever cost an American President his life. The three assassins whose bullets killed Presidents Lincoln, Garfield and McKinley were lonely psychopaths, adrift from history in a morbid fascination with the place history gives those who reverse its orderly progress. Each sought a moment of mad glory—and each died convinced that history would understand."

THE LONE ASSASSIN HYPOTHESIS WOULD have its advocates in Europe, but, by February of 1964, a former American journalist, Thomas J. Buchanan, was already articulating an alternative point of view in the pages of the Paris newspaper, *l'Express*. *Time* magazine's historical assertions were patently false, Buchanan countered. Leon Czolgosz shot and killed President MacKinley for decidedly political reasons. In his own words, the left-wing Czolgosz confessed that he had committed the act "for the good of the working people." His arrest was followed by the wide-scale arrest of fellow anarchists around the country.

There was also the question of Czolgosz's alleged insanity. "No convincing, independent proof of Czolgosz's madness was ever offered," Buchanan wrote. "Nor did any court ever find him insane... An attempt to prove that Czolgosz had accomplices was made, but in the time allowed, no evidence was found to indicate that he did... The trial of Czolgosz was rushed through to its conclusion in eight hours, and the jury found him guilty after a deliberation of precisely 34 minutes. He was then electrocuted, but his executioners did not permit his family to claim

A DALLAS CONSPIRACY?

THOMAS BUCHANAN WAS ONE OF FIVE European correspondents to write early, and well, about the contradictions easily discerned in the case the Dallas authorities had attempted to mount against Lee Harvey Oswald. Published in London early in 1964, Nerin E. Gun's *Red Roses from Texas* has the distinction of being the first published book critical of the official case against Oswald.

Gun's work was followed by Buchanan; Leo Sauvage's writings for both *Commentary* and *Le Figaro*; Hans Habe's *The Wounded Land*, first published by K. Desch in Germany, and Joachim Joesten's study of *Oswald: Assassin or Fall Guy*, first serialized in Opera Mundi European newspaper syndicate starting in March, 1964.

It was Joachim Joesten, for example, a distinquished author active in the Resistance underground during WWII, who first pointed out the mysteries concerning the President's Dallas motorcade route. As Joesten noted, unless Oswald had been

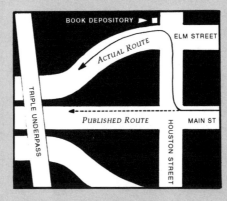

somehow in touch with the Dallas politicians who persuaded President Kennedy to change that route at the last minute, he would have left for work that morning, curtain rod or rifle package in hand, knowing that the President's motorcade would come no closer than a block away from the School Book Depository.

The map of the scheduled motorcade route which appeared in the *Dallas Morning News* on Nov. 22, 1963 clearly showed that the President was scheduled to travel directly down Main Street through the Triple Underpass before picking up Stemmons Freeway for his journey to the Trade Mart for lunch.

If someone had not persuaded the President to make a last minute double detour onto Houston Street, and then directly in front of the Book Depository onto Elm, it would have been impossible for Oswald, or anyone else, to have hit the President from the sixth floor of that building with a $14 mail-order rifle, particularly as the President's car would have been travelling a lot faster than a mere fifteen miles an hour. Unless he had inside knowledge, Joesten concluded, we may have never have heard of Lee Harvey Oswald.

The controversy would grow more bizarre later that year, when the Warren Commission revealed that two Dallas newspapers—including the *News*—printed the actual motorcade route, including detours, several days before the shooting. Which version, if any, had Oswald seen?

The "Mister X" Theory

Thomas Buchanan speculated that a certain "Mr. X.," a right-wing Texas oil millionaire decided to knock off two hated world leaders at once: killing Kennedy in such a way that Nikita Krushchev would be blamed, and ultimately discredited in the eye of world opinion. In addition to "Mr. X," Buchanan listed six other possible members of the plot: (1) the assassin on the Triple Underpass bridge, who may have been Ruby; (2) a second assassin located in the Texas School Book Depository, wearing a police uniform; (3) a police officer involved in Oswald's arrest; (4) Tippit; (5) the Marxist Oswald; (6) another policeman who missed Oswald as he left the building. When Tippit failed to kill Oswald, Mr. X enlisted Jack Ruby at the last minute to do the job. Drawback: Bernard Weissman — the John Birch official who funded the hate Kennedy literature which greeted the President on his arrival — spelled his last name with a "W", and not an "X."

his corpse quite yet. First they poured the contents of a large container of carbolic acid over his dead body, as it lay within the coffin.

"This last gesture—punishing the corpse of the 'insane' assassin," Buchanan adds, tartly, "was, McKinley backers thought, the work of sane men."

As for the assassination of President Garfield, his murderer was a lawyer by the name of Charles J. Guiteau. Guiteau was strongly associated with the extreme right wing of Garfield's own Republican political party. Garfield had been shot for political reasons, so his assassin always acknowledged. With Garfield dead, the right wing had a much easier time once again taking control of the Republican Party.

PRESIDENT ABRAHAM LINCOLN'S ASSASsination provided the most haunting parallels with Kennedy's murder. "Not only did Lincoln's assassin have accomplices on the ground, working with him," Buchanan argued, "he also had accomplices above him, who were never caught and punished. They escaped the scaffold because the one man who could have identified them was silenced. His name was John Wilkes Booth, and he was murdered, like Lee Harvey Oswald, while in the custody of the men who had arrested him."

The "It Could Never Happen Here" mentality, Buchanan, and other early European critics argued, is a fog that will first have to lift before America can fully realize the terrible truth buried in the contradictions of Dealey Plaza.

Thunder on the Right

The John Birch Society Controversy

During the same month that Thomas Buchanan began his series of articles on the role of the Dallas right wing, the John Birch Society came forward with their own theory on the men behind the guns in Dealey Plaza. In the February 1964 edition of *American Opinion*, the Birch Society house organ, an Illinois professor with the unlikely name of Revilo P. Oliver—Revilo is Oliver spelled backwards—laid the entire crime squarely at the feet of the International Communist Conspiracy.

For "The Conspiracy," John Kennedy was simply wandering too far off the reservation. In spite of his phony invasion of Cuba, and his collaboration with Khrushchev on a fake missile crisis, the President was executed for one of two possible reasons, according to Professor Oliver.

1) "The assassination was the result of one of the rifts that not infrequently occur within the management of the Communist conspiracy, whose satraps sometimes liquidate one another

for defecting from the Conspiracy, just as Persian satraps, such as Tissaphernes and Phranabazus, made war on one another without revolting or intending to revolt against the King of Kings."

2) "Kennedy was executed by the Communist Conspiracy because he was planning to turn American."

For this comforting hypothesis, the Professor comments, ironically, "there is no known reason."

Whatever their final reason, the Conspiracy felt

compelled, the Professor continues, "to order the assassination as part of a systematic preparation for a domestic take-over [of America].... The plan was to place the blame on right-wing extremists (the Bolshevik code-word for informed and loyal Americans), and ... a whole train of clues were carefully planted to lead or point in that direction as soon as Oswald was safe in Mexico."

Professor Oliver seemed to be more a big idea man, and did not go into the details of the assassination at great length. Oswald, the Professor claimed, had been trained in sabotage, terrorism and guerilla warfare in the well-known school for international criminals located in Minsk. He was brought back into the United States by officials in the "communist-controlled State Department." He was walking directly toward the apartment of Jakob Rubenstein (alias Jack Ruby) when he was stopped by the police. And, finally, he ordered his rifle by mail "to create propaganda for banning the sale of firearms to the public, and to "reduce the occupation hazards to the Balubas, Outer Mongolians, or other beasts" scheduled to form the "international police force" that will occupy the U.S. after the actual takeover.

It was not Professor Oliver's imaginative theory, however, but rather his pure cold hatred of JFK which eventually got him into hot water with Illinois campus officials.

"So long as there are Americans," Oliver concluded, "Kennedy's memory will be cherished with distaste.... And if the international vermin succeed in completing their occupation of our country, Americans will remember Kennedy while they live, and will curse him as they face the firing squads or toil in brutish degradation."

On the publication of these opinions, protests broke out on the Illinois campus. The protests soon subsided, however, when the student editor of the *Daily Illini*, and burgeoning film buff Roger Ebert wrote "only a strong and free society could permit his own freedom." In the mind of Revilo Oliver, however, the Outer Mongolians were nonetheless still there, standing just outside the wall.

BACK TO BROOKLYN

In early 1964, author/polemicist Morris Beale published a thinly disguised fictional reconstruction of the crime entitled *Guns of the Regressive Right, or How To Kill A President*. A very strange little book, "Guns" has the historical distinction of being the first of a score of novels to deal with the murder of JFK.

In his novel, his tongue thoroughly locked in cheek, the author of those previous unsung classics *Red Rat Race*, *Washington Squirrel Cage*, and *All American Louse: The Biography of Drew Pearson*, describes how Wall Street, or the "Regressive" Right orchestrated the Kennedy assassination to discredit the forces of Harry Silverton [Barry Goldwater: get it?] and the "Realist" Right from taking over the fortunes and future of the Republican Party.

The conspiracy is first put into motion at the House of Dockstader, located at 666 Wall Street in New York City. The Chairman of the plot is 82 year old Jasper Jarrell, "six decades out of Tishomingo, Oklahoma, the patriarchal head of "Amalgamated Oil."

Jarrell (Rockefeller) explains the problem to his committee in the following manner: "We have been unable to make a deal with Silverton to have him turn all authority in the high echelons of government over to us—as young Joe Smith (Kennedy) and as Mickey Eisenheimer (Ike, of course) did before him—and it looks like we will not be able to take over Smith or Silverton by this means."

Jarrell then turns to mass media magnate Greeley Pulitzer to provide the solution. "We will kill young Joe Smith with a bullet, and we will kill Harry Silverton with newspaper propaganda created and concocted with that bullet. We will step up the vilification of the John Spruce Society and we will build up an image of Silverton as the personification of the Sprucites. The 1,800 odd member newspapers of the Amalgamated Press will do their part even more. I'll see that slanted and even phony news is put on the wire and teletype in ever increasing quantities."

Like a badly-executed, sophomoric *Spy* magazine spoof, "Operation History" is thus set into motion. The best marksmen in the Communist world, Samokov Tata, is hired as the real triggerman. A young Marxist from New York City, Grant Osteen, is hired as the decoy. When Osteen is captured after the shooting, Jarrell turns to his old friend, Reggio Lucca for help. Lucca, who has a narcotics drop in Dallas, in turn hires a Chicago-bred, Dallas mob boy by the name of Beanie Bimstein to eliminate Osteen. Tata is himself later murdered on board an escape boat out in the Caribbean.

All in all, "Operation History" is a great success. Smith is dead. Silverton will never be elected President. And Smith's actual successor, former Senator Lynn Jonas, from the State of Texas, is the kind of political hack that the House of Dockstader has always been able to control.

As literary parodies go, it is possible, though not easy, to find books less imaginative than Morris Beale's *Guns of the Regressive Right*. The one truly transcendent moment in the novel occurs in the coda where the ghost of Sam Houston sits down with the ghost of Wilbert Robinson, the former manager of the Brooklyn Dodgers!

"What's this news from Dallas—mah Home state," General Houston roared at Uncle Robbie. "It's the ding-dangdest thing I ever heerd of. Was there ever a screwier city, or was there ever a city that got itself so screwed up."

"Yes," said Uncle Robbie. "Brooklyn. When I was there."

The George Bush Young Republicans Theory

On November 22, 1963, Houston FBI Agent Graham W. Kitchell was contacted "telephonically" by Mr. George H. W. Bush, 5525 Briar, Houston. The future President had some hearsay to relate. He advised Kitchell that one James Parrott had been talking of killing the President when he came to Houston. Contacted by the FBI, Parrott advised the FBI that Yes, he was a member of the Young Republicans, and Yes, he had picketed members of the the Kennedy administration when they came to Texas. A fellow young Republican, Kerney Reynolds, confirmed that Parrott had, however, been in Houston all day, and could not have killed President Kennedy. There is no information to suggest that Mr. Bush had been in direct contact with Jasper Jarrell at any time immediately leading up to the President's assassination.

Thunder on the Right

The Trial of Jack Ruby

The Jack Ruby Sanity Controversy

Jack Ruby—the man who murdered the man said to have murdered John Fitzgerald Kennedy—went on trial in Judge Joe R. Brown's Dallas courtroom on February 17, 1964. Having executed Lee Harvey Oswald in the basement of the Dallas Police Station, before live television cameras, Ruby, the 53 year-old proprietor of a local striptease parlor, was not expected to mount much of a defense.

Nicknamed "Sparky" in childhood for his violent temper, Ruby claimed that Oswald's "sarcastic sneer" had caused him to snap. He had shot "the rat," as the world had plainly seen, in a spontaneous act of retribution some would consider traditional as for the administration of justice on the old wild western frontier.

For Jack Ruby's lawyer, Melvin Belli of San Francisco, himself somewhat of an old-fashioned Frisco Dandy, what this proved was that his client had gone bonkers. Ruby, in short, was nuts. Pleading that his brain-damaged client had been overcome by an epileptic seizure, Belli begged the court for mercy.

In an episode as seedy as most of those which had gone before, after a jury deliberation which lasted all of two hours and nineteen minutes, Ruby was found guilty of first degree murder on March 14, 1964.

In truth, Sparky never really had much of a chance. One of America's finest journalists, Murray Kempton, covered Ruby's trial with sympathy that spring in 1964, in the pages of the *New Republic*, and *The (London) Spectator*.

"Ruby sits now," Kempton wrote in *The Spectator*, "in an apple-green washed courtroom under two generation old, post pre-Raphaelite frescoes—one of the Lady Justice and one of Lady Freedom. These two Ladies have the pinched mouths and sad eyes we associate with the Dallas women who spat on Adlai Stevenson. Lady Freedom's torch seems to be waiting for a school to burn. Jack Ruby is being tried by Judge Joe R. Brown, whose notions of aesthetics, dignity and humour were summarised in the moment when he looked at the proportions of these two desiccated vestals and observed to the international press that 'Justice is better built than Freedom.'"

For Murray Kempton, the Jack Ruby trial soon became a bad joke. "This was a case great only because it was notorious. It was managed without dignity from the bench, without concentration from the defense table, without even usual effort from the prosecution, which used its natural advantages skillfully enough, but had altogether so easy a time that, we are told, District Attorney Henry Wade intended to petition the governor for a commutation of the sentence because "he felt that Ruby had not received a proper defense."

"In point of fact," Kempton wrote, "Ruby received no defense at all; the impression is inescapable that Mr. Belli made himself the defendant almost at once, that District Attorney Wade and his assistants happily accepted him as such; and that, at the end, when the jury ordered Ruby to the block, Belli was more an object of its disfavor than his client."

THE ESSENCE OF BELLI'S DEFENSE SEEMED TO have been that, yes, his client was insane, but it was the city of Dallas itself which finally drove Sparky over the edge. While this point of view might find champions across America, it was not a strategy which could be expected to find that much support among an all-white, entirely Protestant, hometown jury. Dallas lawyer Tom Howard summed up the spirit of the place when he said "the Ruby trial was just another nigger murder case [best] handled among us Dallasites."

"Every city gets the immigrants it deserves," Murray Kempton concluded. "Jack Ruby came here from Chicago. When he tried to go into business for himself, he began with the Interlude, a restaurant to which he hoped that established and successful citizens would bring their wives. And, when that did not do so well, he started the Carousel, where he hoped that at least upwardly-mobile junior executives might find a place to pursue their office infidelities. When that failed, he was reduced to putting in the strip teasers.

"It is said that things are different in Europe—a culture perhaps less dominated by amateurs—but, in the American enterprise of entertainment, there is no rung below that occupied by the strip parlour. No one who has experienced the transient loneliness of being a customer in one of them could ever think without a pang of the permanent loneliness of being its proprietor."

UNANSWERED QUESTIONS

The trial of Jack Ruby concluded without shedding new light on a possible conspiracy in the assassination of President Kennedy. Both the prosecution and the defense chose to ignore details which seemed to suggest a much wider plot.

On the day Ruby shot Oswald, for example, a magician-ventriloquist by the name of Billy De Mar—whose real name was William D. Crowe, Jr.—was quoted by the Associated Press as saying that Oswald had been a patron of Jack Ruby's Carousel Club. De Mar had worked at the Carousel, and claimed that Oswald had been in the club as recently as nine days before the President's assassination. At least fourteen other witnesses would also place Oswald at the Carousel in the months leading up to the killings.

None of these reports were cited, however, during the course of the Ruby trial.

Ruby's relationship with members of the Dallas Police Force was another issue of profound curiosity, at least to the international press. The fact that Ruby had attended the Wade press conference; had been inside Parkland when the President was rushed there after the shooting; and had access to the Dallas Police station on the day he shot Oswald raised important questions about Ruby's insider status with the police. The majority of Dallas police present at the shooting of Oswald, for example, knew Jack Ruby by name.

Finally, there was the question of Ruby's general affiliation with mobsters he had known, and worked with, since his early days on the streets of Chicago. As a child, Ruby had run errands for Al Capone. He often bragged about his affection and respect for California gangster Mickey Cohen.

Much more urgently, in Dallas, Ruby had at times openly been affiliated with members of the New Orleans-based Carlos Marcello gang family, the Trafficante family in Havana and pre-Castro Cuba, and with Murray "Dusty" Miller, a Jimmy Hoffa Teamster official in Texas. Miller would himself later turn up as George Bush's union liaison in Bush's 1980 Senatorial campaign. In the public's mind, however, from the time of his trial in 1964 until his death in January 1967, Ruby was portrayed as a crazed loner—much like the man he killed, Lee Harvey Oswald.

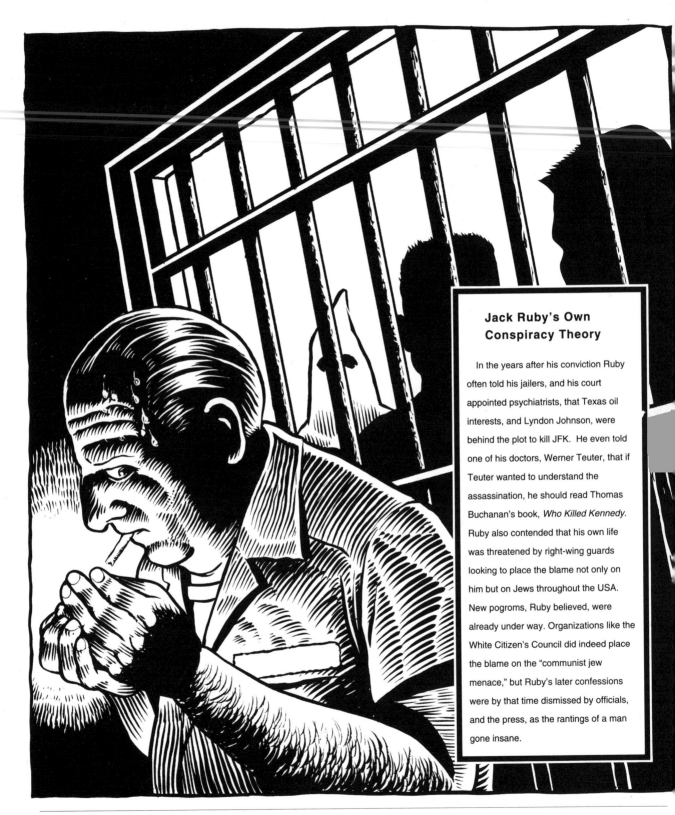

Jack Ruby's Own Conspiracy Theory

In the years after his conviction Ruby often told his jailers, and his court appointed psychiatrists, that Texas oil interests, and Lyndon Johnson, were behind the plot to kill JFK. He even told one of his doctors, Werner Teuter, that if Teuter wanted to understand the assassination, he should read Thomas Buchanan's book, *Who Killed Kennedy*. Ruby also contended that his own life was threatened by right-wing guards looking to place the blame not only on him but on Jews throughout the USA. New pogroms, Ruby believed, were already under way. Organizations like the White Citizen's Council did indeed place the blame on the "communist jew menace," but Ruby's later confessions were by that time dismissed by officials, and the press, as the rantings of a man gone insane.

The Official Story

The Warren Report Single Bullet Controversy

The conviction of Jack Ruby was taken as a signal by the Warren Commission to begin its formal field investigation into the death of President Kennedy. From mid-March until the first of June, 1964, staff lawyers from the Commission descended upon Dallas to evaluate the huge and often contradictory body of evidence which had been supplied to them by their sole investigative arm, J. Edgar Hoover's Federal Bureau of Investigation.

By mid-June, less than three months after it began, the independent phase of the investigation was over, and most of the senior lawyers assigned to the investigation by chief counsel J. Lee Rankin had returned to their private law practices. Rankin and three key aides, Norman Redlich, Howard Willens and Alfred Goldberg, were now left with the task of preparing the final report for September publication.

Named for its chairman, revered Supreme Court Chief Justice Earl Warren, the Commission was appointed by President Lyndon B. Johnson on November 29, 1963, six days after Kennedy's murder. The State of Texas, the House of Representatives, and the Senate were all preparing independent investigations when President Johnson appointed his own Presidential Commission.

IN ADDITION TO THE CHIEF JUSTICE, THE COMmission included two prominent members of the US Senate—Democrat Richard Russell of Georgia, and Republican John Sherman Cooper of Kentucky; two prominent members from the House—Republican Gerald Ford of Michigan and Democrat Hale Boggs of Louisiana, and two very spooky East Coast Establishment types—John J. McCloy, former head of the World Bank, and Allen Dulles, former director of the CIA. Throughout its proceedings, Ford, McCloy and Dulles would function as an unofficial rump wing of the Commission, uniquely sensitive to questions of national security.

The Report, however, was almost entirely staff crafted. Most of the Commissioners had next to nothing to do with its actual preparation. Several of the commissioners showed a tendency to skip many of the investigative hearings, unless a particularly well-publicized witness, such as Marina Oswald, was testifying.

On September 24, 1964, the Commission released its final 888 page report. While the complete transcripts of the hearings would eventually run to 26 volumes, the essence of the Report was summed up in twelve primary conclusions contained in the opening pages of the initial volume.

The first set of three interlocking points addressed the basic facts of the assassination. These conclusions were based on the investigations of assistant counsel Arlen Specter, an assistant district attorney in Philadelphia who had come to Washington to work for the Commission.

A future senator from Pennsylvania, who would one day achieve an added degree of notoriety for his bristly cross-examination of Oklahoma law professor Anita Hill, Arlen Specter's work for the Warren Commission placed him at the center of considerable controversy.

As initially advanced by Specter, the Commission's first conclusion addressed the source of the fatal shots. "The shots which killed President Kennedy, and wounded Governor Connally," the Report stated, "were fired from the sixth floor window at the southeast corner of the Texas School Book Depository." The Commission offered the following six assertions of evidence as the basis for this conclusion:

"(1) Witnesses at the scene of the assassination saw a rifle being fired from the sixth floor window of the Depository Building, and some witnesses saw a rifle in the window immediately after the shots were fired.

"(2) The nearly whole bullet found on Governor Connally's stretcher at Parkland Memorial Hospital and the two bullet fragments found in the front seat of the Presidential limousine were fired from the 6.5 millimeter Mannlicher-Carcano rifle found on the sixth floor of the Depository Building to the exclusion of all other weapons.

"(3) The three used cartridge cases found near the window on the sixth floor at the southeast corner of the building were fired from the same rifle which fired the above-described bullet and fragments to the exclusion of all other weapons.

"(4) The windshield in the Presidential limousine was struck by a bullet fragment on the inside surface of the glass, but was not penetrated.

"(5) The nature of the bullet wound suffered by President Kennedy and Governor Connally," the Report continued, "and the location of the car at the time of shots establish that bullets were fired from above and behind the Presidential limousine, striking the President and the Governor as follows:

1) President Kennedy was first struck by a bullet which entered at the back of his neck and exited through the lower front portion of his neck, causing a wound which would not necessarily have been lethal. The President was struck a second time by a bullet which entered the right-rear portion of his head causing a massive and fatal wound.

2) Governor Connally was struck by a bullet which entered on the right side of his chest, exiting below his right nipple. This bullet then passed through his right wrist and entered his left thigh where it caused a superficial wound."

"(6) There is no credible evidence that the shots were fired from the Triple Underpass, ahead of the motorcade,

The Official Story

or from any other location."

The second and third conclusions reached by the Warren Commission both flowed neatly enough out of the scenario described in the first.

The second conclusion was quite brief.

"The weight of the evidence indicates there were three shots fired."

The third and final conclusion, however, was a minor masterpiece of legal obfuscation. The deliberately awkward and tentative language found in this final paragraph would ultimately fail to camouflage a controversy which would undermine the authority of this supposedly definitive investigation in the days to come.

"Although it is not necessary to any essential findings of the Commission to determine just which shot hit Governor Connally, there is very persuasive evidence from the experts to indicate that the same bullet which pierced the President's throat also caused Governor Connally's wounds," the Report stated. *"However, Governor Connally's testimony and certain other factors have given rise to some difference of opinion as to this probability, but there is no question in the mind of any member of the Commission that all the shots which caused the President's and Governor Connally's wounds were fired from the sixth floor window of the Texas School Book Depository.*

THE SINGLE BULLET THEORY

As developed by Arlen Specter, the Single Bullet Theory was the only way the Warren Commission could explain the assassination in terms of a lone assassin. The Warren Commission had already concluded that Kennedy was killed by a bullet fired from a 6.5 Mannlicher-Carcano rifle. A bolt action rifle, the Mannlicher takes a minimum of 2.3 seconds to lock, load, and fire. The Zapruder film, however, shows conclusively that no more than 1.7 seconds elapsed between the time the first bullet hit Kennedy, and the first bullet hit Connally. Kennedy and Connally had to have been hit by the same bullet, as the Mannlicher-Carcano rifleman simply did not have enough time to fire another round. Unless, of course, somebody else was firing into the Presidential limousine at the same time. Add the evidence up another way, and you get at least two gunmen. The ultimate authority of the Warren Commission, and the truth of who killed JFK, rested then and still rests, on what may or may not have happened in Dallas during those critical point six (.6) seconds.

The Commission had a real problem on its hands in advancing this conclusion. By the time this paragraph was composed, the Commissioners already knew that one bullet had killed the President, and that another shot had missed the Presidential limousine entirely.

If the limitations of Oswald's rifle left him time to fire only three bullets, then this left only one other bullet to account for, and that bullet *had* to have been the one that passed through Kennedy's neck, Connally's chest, wrist, and finally into the Governor's thigh—causing seven distinct wounds—before it was eventually recovered more or less intact on a stretcher in Parkland Hospital.

Either this bullet had followed that exact yet improbable flight pattern, or a fourth bullet would have to have been fired, probably from some location other than the sixth floor of the Book Depository.

The trajectory of this single, devastating bullet became the linch pin for the entire Report. Pull the pin out, and the entire Warren Report collapsed like some fragile Rube Goldberg practical science project.

The Rifleman

The Marksmanship Controversy

Having chronicled "the basic facts of the assassination," the Warren Commission Report next took up the question of the rifleman and his weapon. On this point, the Commissioners were emphatic: "The shots which killed President Kennedy and wounded Governor Connally were fired by Lee Harvey Oswald." The Commissioners listed seven subconclusions to support this assertion:

"*(1) The Mannlicher-Carcano 6.5 Italian rifle from which the shots were fired was owned by and in the possession of Oswald.*

"*(2) Oswald carried this rifle into the Depository Building on the morning of November 22, 1963.*

"*(3) Oswald, at the time of the assassination, was present at the window from which the shots were fired.*

"*(4) Shortly after the assassination,* the Mannlicher-Carcano rifle belonging to Oswald was found partially hidden between some cartons on the sixth floor and the improvised paper bag in which Oswald brought the rifle to the Depository was found close by the window from which the shots were fired.*

"*(5) Based on testimony of the experts and their analysis of films of the assassination, the Commission has concluded that a rifleman of Lee Harvey Oswald's capabilities could have fired the shots from the rifle used in the assassination within the elapsed time of the shooting. The Commission has concluded further that Oswald possessed the capability with a rifle which enabled him to to commit the assassination.*

"*(6) Oswald lied to the police after his arrest concerning important substantive matters.*

"*(7) Oswald had attempted to kill Maj. Gen. Edwin A. Walker (Resigned, U.S. Army) on April 10, 1963, thereby demonstrating his disposition to take human life.*"

And yet, at the time of the Report's release, the Commission had gathered evidence which undercut at least six of these seven sub-conclusions. First of all, Oswald had carried something into the Depository that morning, but the eyewitnesses who informed the Commission of this fact also maintained that the package was too small to contain a rifle of the size of the Mannlicher-Carcano.

THE key DEALEY PLAZA eyewitness, Howard Brennan, claimed to have looked up from the street to see Oswald at the window of the sixth floor, but Brennan later allowed that he would be unable to pick Oswald out of a police line-up.

The fiber analysis which linked the rifle to the paper bag found on the sixth floor, moreover, was considered "inconclusive" by the Commission's own scientific analysts.

The Commission's remaining sub-conclusions suffered under the weight of similar scrutiny. Oswald may very well have lied to the police after his arrest, but, wildly enough, the Dallas Police had failed to keep a transcript of this interrogation, so there was no evidence whatsoever concerning what was said during those critical sessions.

The most improbable of all of these sub-conclusions concerned the business of Oswald's—or anyone else's—ability to have killed Kennedy using a weapon like the Mannlicher-Carcano under such circumstances. Because of its faulty scope, neither FBI nor US Army sharpshooters were ever able to duplicate Oswald's alleged "accomplishment." The Commission's case was not improved when it was also learned that, as a Marine, Oswald tested as no better than an average marksman.

The Commission did, however, make at least one point which has linked Lee Harvey Oswald to the crime ever since. A Texas School Book Depository employee, with regular access to the sixth floor, Oswald did own the gun which fired the bullets that wounded Governor Connally, and which left bullet fragments in and around the Presidential limousine. Almost completely intact, another bullet of the type used by Oswald's rifle, was found at Parkland Hosptial. While critics of the Report have often theorized that somebody else may have fired Oswald's rifle that fatal day, in the intervening thirty years no one has yet introduced direct evidence to support this assertion.

THE MANNLICHER-CARCANO

ON THE MORNING OF NOVEMBER 27, 1963, FBI Agent Robert Frazier found himself on a local firing range with the rifle that had allegedly killed President Kennedy in his hands. His assignment that morning was simple, though the most important of his career: test the rifle to see if Oswald could have actually made those shots.

During the course of the morning Frazier and two other FBI agents, Charles Killion and Courtland Cunningham, all tested the gun for accuracy. Each agent fired three shots with the Mannlicher. All nine shots were high and to the right. And the agents had been aiming at a stationary target only fifteen feet away.

The time it took to make these shots was very important. None of the men were able to get off all three shots in the time it had taken to hit Kennedy.

That afternoon, Frazier conducted still another test: How fast could this gun be fired, Frazier wondered, if you just forgot about the target and simply fired the weapon as fast as you could?

Once again Frazier employed a three bullet test. The first set took four point eight seconds (4.8) to fire. The second series, four point six seconds (4.6). It was possible, therefore to fire the weapon as fast as Oswald would have needed to twice hit Kennedy, Frazier learned—but only if you didn't hesitate to aim.

In conducting tests with Oswald's rifle, Frazier had stumbled upon another truth every bit as disturbing as the question of accuracy. The rifle was bolt action, not an automatic. Allowing for the time it would take to place a round in the chamber, fire, eject the cartridge, and load the next bullet, it was impossible to fire the gun without an absolute minimum of two point three seconds (2.3) between shots.

At the time Frazier noted this, interval timing wasn't a matter of vital significance. But eventually, when the firing tests were stacked up against the Zapruder film, this contradiction became essential to the Warren Commission. If all the bullets couldn't be traced to Oswald's rifle, the Commission had a conspiracy on its hands. It was left to Arlen Specter to solve this dilemma.

Oswald's Mannlicher-Carcano would be tested by Frazier once again the following March, and then it would be the U.S. Army's turn with the rifle. In spite of the Warren Report's assertion that "a rifleman of Oswald's capabilities could have fired the shots from the rifle used in the assassination within the elapsed time of the shooting" the Commission never found a marksman from either the FBI, or the U.S. Army, able to duplicate those shots.

A Most Violent Man

The "Motive for the Crime" Controversy

With its reconstruction of "the basic facts of the assassination" hanging on the flight pattern of a very special bullet, and with serious questions raised as to whether its declared assassin was even present on the sixth floor of the Texas School Book Depository, the Warren Commission clearly needed more convincing detail to cement its case against Lee Harvey Oswald.

Well, what about Oswald's motive? Research suggested that if anything, Oswald had a stronger motive for taking a shot at Texas Governor John Connally, who, as former head of the Navy department, had denied Oswald an honorable discharge from military service. Most of those testifying to Oswald's character claimed he deeply admired President Kennedy. Concerning motive, it would have been easier to make the case that Oswald was aiming at Connally on Nov. 22, 1963.

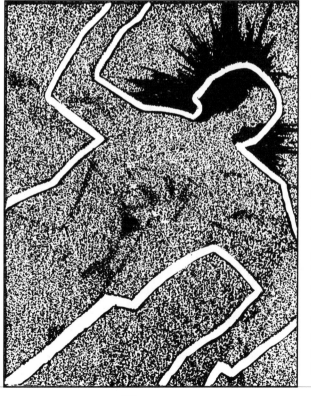

The Commission realized, however, that it had to say something about a possible motive, so it listed the following five factors which it believed predisposed Oswald to attempt assassination: 1) Oswald's hostility to his environment, 2) his failure to establish meaningful relationships, 3) his desire to find a place in history, 4) his commitment to Marxism and Communism, and 5) his capacity to act decisively without regard to the consequences.

On reading these assertions one Commission lawyer complained to a colleague that the list read like a series of cliches from a TV soap opera. As Murray Kempton would later point out, the Commission had launched this small exercise into psychopathology without the advantage of having even one professional psychologist on its staff. It had been

A Most Violent Man

left to amateur shrinks such as Gerald Ford and Allen Dulles to plumb the depths of Lee Harvey Oswald's mind.

Without a convincing motive, the Commission turned instead to Oswald's alleged record of violent crime. The murder of Dallas policeman Jefferson Davis Tippit became, for at least one staff lawyer, David Belin, "the rosetta stone" which proved that Oswald was the President's assassin.

"Oswald killed Dallas Police Patrolman J.D. Tippit approximately 45 minutes after the assassination," the Report concluded. "[Moreover] this conclusion upholds the finding that Oswald fired the shots which killed President Kennedy and wounded Governor Connally and is supported by the following:

(1) Two eyewitnesses saw the Tippit shooting and seven eyewitnesses heard the shots and saw the gunman leave the scene with revolver in hand. These nine eyewitnesses positively identified Lee Harvey Oswald as the man they saw.

(2) The cartridge cases found at the scene of the shooting were fired from the revolver in the possession of Oswald at the time of his arrest to the exclusion of all other weapons.

THE TALKING GENERAL WALKER BLUES

FOR THE WARREN COMMISSION, Oswald's assassination of President Kennedy was in part explained by both his subsequent murder of Officer Tippit, and his previous attempt on the life of retired US Army General Edwin A. Walker on April 10, 1963—seven months before Dealey Plaza. On the night of the 10th, as the General sat in his study, a bullet crashed through his window, and narrowly missed taking the General's life.

Although this case was considered unsolved by Texas officials at the time, the Commission broke ground by announcing to the world that Oswald had been the shooter.

Once again the Commission's conclusion flew in the face of the available evidence. For one thing, an eyewitness to the event saw two men fleeing from the scene of the crime. Since this allegation implied that Oswald on occasion took on accomplices in his crimes, it would have been good of the Commission if it had spent any time trying to figure out that accomplice's identity. Perhaps no one bothered because the cartridge shells retrieved at Walker's home did not match Oswald's rifle.

The case against Oswald as Walker's potential assassin had been made almost entirely by Marina Oswald during the course of her four different appearances at the Hearings. She told the Commission that her husband had also attempted to take the life of then former Vice President, Richard Nixon. The Commission knew her testimony was wildly erratic and next to worthless. "Marina Oswald has lied to the Secret Service, the FBI, and to this Commission on matters of vital concern," staff lawyer Norman Redlich asserted as early as February, 1964. And yet, in September, the Commission was more than willing to use that testimony to connect Oswald to General Walker.

TWENTY-FOUR YEARS LATER, IN A 1988 interview in *Ladies Home Journal*, Marina Oswald finally recanted her testimony. "When I was questioned by the Warren Commission, I was a blind kitten," she said. "Their questioning left me only one way to go: guilty. I made Lee guilty. He never had a fair chance. But I was only 22 then, and I've matured since; I think differently."

Marina Oswald went on to say that she felt she had to tell the Commission what they wanted to hear, or risk being deported. By 1988 she had come to believe that her husband was a patsy in a larger government and organized crime conspiracy to kill the President of the United States.

(3) The revolver in Oswald's possession at the time of his arrest was purchased by and belonged to Oswald.

(4) Oswald's jacket was found along the path of flight taken by the gunman as he fled from the scene of the killing."

Once again, however, the Commission bypassed the contradictions inherent in the evidence they themselves had gathered, offering instead a misleading selection of evidence carefully orchestrated to place Lee Harvey Oswald in a most sinister light.

The Commission had, in fact, only two eyewitnesses to the actual crime, and one of these eyewitnesses, Domingo Benavides, told the police that he was unable to identify the killer. The testimony of the other eyewitness, Helen Lousie Markham, was so riddled by impossibilities that one Warren staff lawyer described it as "worthless."

The cartridge issue also had its problems. Having personally marked two of the cartridge cases at the scene of the crime, Officer J.M. Poe was later unable to find those markings when asked to identify them by the FBI. According to Officer Poe, the cartridge cases presented by the FBI did not match up with the shells he had found next to Tippit's body.

The remaining two subconclusions were equally inconclusive.

Lee Harvey Oswald may very well have been the man who killed Officer Tippit; but based on the evidence the Commission offered in its Report, it is highly unlikely that this particular assertion, like so many before it, would have ever stood up in court, if subjected to the normal challenges of an adversary system of justice. A sky full of reasonable doubts now hung over the Commission's Report like an autumn thunder storm about to blow through Dogpatch.

The Ring Around the Collar Theory

According to Edward Jay Epstein, it was George de Mohrenschildt, an Oswald family friend with U.S. Intelligence connections, who first advanced the theory that marital discord may have played a part in the murder of JFK. According to de Mohrenschildt, the night before the assassination, Marina Oswald told her husband that she simply could not live with him any longer "unless he was willing to equip their apartment with a washing machine." A bitter fight followed, which left Oswald in the mood to hurt somebody bad. For Epstein, the theory seems quite unlikely because, among other reasons, there was a pretty good laundromat right around the corner.

A Most Violent Man

The Question of Conspiracy

The Warren Report Lone Gunman Controversy

Having made its case against Lee Harvey Oswald, the Commission next took up the question of whether Oswald had assistance in killing JFK. In three final conclusions, the Commissioners made the case that both Oswald, and Jack Ruby, had acted alone.

"The Commission has found no evidence that either Lee Harvey Oswald or Jack Ruby was part of any conspiracy, domestic or foreign, to assassinate President Kennedy," the Report stated.

Additionally, "in its entire investigation the Commission has found no evidence of conspiracy, subversion, or disloyalty to the US Government by any Federal, State, or local official."

And, finally, "on the basis of the evidence before the Commission it concludes that Oswald acted alone."

In reaching these conclusions the Commission was responding in part to the early criticism and theories of Mark Lane, Thomas Buchanan, Joachim Joesten and Leo Sauvage. The Commission also was operating under incredi-

ble political pressure from both FBI Director J. Edgar Hoover, and President Lyndon B. Johnson, to make its case against Lee Harvey Oswald as the lone assassin at the earliest possible opportunity.

In a now familiar series of subconclusions, the Commission listed the basis for its findings. Claiming to have thoroughly investigated, "among other factors, the circumstances surrounding the planning of the motorcade route through Dallas, the hiring of Oswald by the Texas School Book Depository Co. on October 15, 1963, the method by which the rifle was brought into the building, the placing of cartons of books at the window, Oswald's escape from the building, and the testimony of eyewitnesses to the shooting," the Commission concluded that it had "found no evidence that anyone assisted Oswald in planning or carrying out the assassination."

Having thoroughly investigated, "in addition to other possible leads, all facts of Oswald's associations, finances, and personal habits, particularly during the period following his return from the Soviet Union in June, 1962," the Commission concluded that Oswald was not involved "with any person or group in a conspiracy to assassinate the President."

Having reviewed "the circumstances surrounding Oswald's defection to the Soviet Union, his life there from October, 1959 to June, 1962 so far as it can be reconstructed, his known contacts with the Fair Play for Cuba Committee, and his visits to the Cuban and Soviet Embassies in Mexico City during his trip to Mexico from September to October 1963, and his contacts with the Soviet Embassy in the United States," the Commission concluded that Oswald was not "employed, persuaded or encouraged by any foreign government" in the assassination.

By adding the phrase "so far as it can be reconstructed" to its conclusion concerning Oswald's life in the Soviet Union, the Commission did leave itself

Some Critical Words about the Dallas Police

The Warren Commission concluded its Report by taking up the question of Dallas police and Secret Service presidential protection. The Report criticizes the Dallas police on two accounts. The "uninhibited access" allowed to newspaper, radio and television reporters, the Commissioners concluded, subjected Oswald "to harassment and [created] chaotic conditions which were not conducive to orderly interrogation or the protection of the rights of the prisoner."

Secondly, "the numerous statements, sometimes erroneous, made to the press by various local law enforcement officials, during this period of confusion and disorder in the police station, would have presented serious obstacles to the obtaining of a fair trial for Oswald."

On the other hand, the Commission concluded that the Dallas police had treated Oswald in an appropriate manner. "Except for the force required to effect his arrest, Oswald was not subjected to any physical coercion by any law enforcement officials. He was advised that he could not be compelled to give any information and that any statements made by him might be used against him in court. He was advised of his right to counsel. He was given opportunity to obtain counsel of his choice and was offered legal assistance by the Dallas Bar Association, which he rejected at the time."

The Commission failed to mention, however, that the transcripts of Oswald's interrogation sessions, upon which such a conclusion might presumably be based, had been mysteriously lost or destroyed, and were not available to the Warren Commission during the course of their investigation.

Finally, the Commission mildly faulted the Secret

Service for not properly examining threats against the President before arriving in Dallas, for not working closely enough with the FBI to isolate potential troublemakers, and for not inspecting the buildings along the motorcade route for the presence of a potential assassin. The Commission hoped that the Secret Service would incorporate these changes in their protection in the future.

The Question of Conspiracy

The Friendly Fire Theory

In his 1992 book, *Mortal Error*, Bonar Menninger argues that JFK was actually killed by Secret Service agent George Hickey, who accidentally discharged his AR-15 in Kennedy's direction after Lee Harvey Oswald had fired the first two shots at Kennedy from the Texas School Book Depository window. Menninger based his book on the research of ballistics expert Howard Donahue who firmly believes that the way Kennedy's head was positioned, the fatal bullet must have moved on a trajectory roughly equal to the grade of the street. When he accidentally discharged his weapon, Hickey was riding in a Secret Service limousine (code-name "Halfback") directly behind the limousine carrying the Connallys and the Kennedys. Neither the Secret Service or now-retired Agent Hickey have chosen to comment on this theory.

an open door for future revelations as to Oswald perhaps being a tool of the KGB.

Exploring all of Oswald's attempts "to identify himself with various political groups, including the Communist Party of the USA; the Fair Play for Cuba Committee, and the Socialist Workers Party," the Commission stated that the contacts Oswald had initiated with each of these groups were not related to "Oswald's subsequent assassination of the President."

The Commission attempted to shut the door on controversial speculation that Oswald had maintained contact with and been a working asset of various US Intelligence operations, by stating that "there was nothing to support the speculation that Oswald was an agent, employee or informant of the FBI, the CIA, or any other government agency.

"All contacts with Oswald by any of these agencies," the Commission stated, in an eye-catching manner, "were made in the regular exercise of their different responsibilities."

THE COMMISSION COMPLETED THIS SET OF findings by concluding that Oswald did not know Ruby, that Ruby had also acted alone, and that the rumors which claimed that Officer Tippit had been seen drinking at the Carousel Club with both Ruby and Oswald in the months leading up to the assassination were simply untrue.

The entire Warren Report could be summarized in three simple propositions.

(1) John Kennedy had been killed by rifle fire from the southeast corner of the Texas School Book Depository Building.

(2) Lee Harvey Oswald was the rifleman.

(3) Lee Harvey Oswald, and the man who killed him, Jack Ruby, both acted alone.

It was all quite neat, and clearly fit the needs of a wounded nation seeking closure.

All the News That's Fit to Print

The New York Times Controversy

Publication of the Warren Commission Report on September 24, 1964 was greeted by all the major American newspapers, news magazines, and television networks with sustained applause, and heartfelt approval. It was as if a mammoth national nightmare had finally come to an end, and the American people could finally rest their collective consciousness on a pillow of blessed reassurance.

"The Report is amazing in its detail, remarkable in its judicial caution and restraint, yet utterly convincing in all of its major conclusions," *Time* proclaimed in its October 2, 1964 issue. "The evidence against Lee Harvey Oswald is overwhelming, and beyond reasonable doubt."

Life was even more lavish in its praise. "The Report is

a great public document that reflects credit on its author, and the nation it represents," columnist Loudon Wainwright wrote, in the October 16, 1964 issue. "The Report is a tremendously scrupulous document—the most conscientious documentation of facts I have ever read," Wainwright stated.

Newsweek was equally approving, if somewhat more restrained. "In the weight of its evidence," the magazine editorialized, "in its fresh and authentic detail, and the sheer scope, intensity and thoroughness of the investigation revealed in its pages, [the Report] is calm, measured, and overwhelming."

The Warren Report found its greatest advocate, however, in its partnership with the *New York Times*. Publishing the entire Report in a special 48 page supplement on September 28, 1964,

The Times declared that "comprehensive and convincing, the facts [have been] exhaustively gathered, independently checked, cogently set forward, and destroy the basis for the conspiracy theories that have grown weedlike in the country and abroad."

Three days after publishing the Report as a special supplement, *The Times* entered into agreement with Bantam Books, and published a paperback version of the Report which eventually sold more than a million copies.

The Times was not through with this Warren Report business quite yet. In December of 1964, it followed the success of its co-publication of the Report with a second paperback volume called *The Witnesses*.

The Witnesses was sold as "the highlights of the Hearings before the Warren Commission... selected and edited by the *New York Times*." Much like the original Report, the new book was indeed carefully edited to present only those selections which supported the Commission's findings, while at the same time excluding those experts whose testimony might be read as inconsistent with the Commission's final conclusions.

As pointed out by Sylvia Meagher, a New York City public health administrator turned dogged JFK conspiracy researcher, the excerpts from Abraham Zapruder's testimony did not include his stated belief that the shots came from behind him (the grassy knoll). Nor did the testimony of Commander J.J. Humes contain his admission that he destroyed

THE PROSECUTION RESTS

In the months immediately following the publication of the Warren Report, most of the critical monthly news magazines followed the popular press in their praise for the Warren Report.

Writing in the pages of the November 2, 1964 issue of *The Nation*, Stanford law professor Herbert L. Packer declared "the Warren Commission has admirably fulfilled its central objective by producing an account of the circumstances under which President Kennedy was assassinated that is adequate to satisfy all reasonable doubts about the immediate, essential facts."

Professor Packer did, however, wonder aloud how the reader was supposed to resolve the major inconsistencies and contradictions found in the testimony of key witnesses without having access to the 26 volumes of testimony which were not issued, as originally planned, at the same time as the publication of the

Report. Without these volumes, as the professor noted, the reader was left with no adequate way to evaluate the Commission's fact finding process.

To EVALUATE THE REPORT, the *New Republic* turned again to New York journalist Murray Kempton, who had already written sagely about the trial of Jack Ruby for the magazine.

For Kempton, the question of Oswald's marksmanship was only one issue where the evidence gathered by the Commission seemed to suggest an entirely different finding than the conclusion the Commission ultimately reached.

"The Commission accepts without question that the probability of [Oswald] hitting the target was relatively high," Kempton writes. And yet, "if the tests indicate anything," Kempton remarks, "it is that the

probability of Oswald hitting the target was rather low."

"In the face of all the other evidence, I am ready to concede," Kempton writes, "that Oswald might just this once have been functioning over his head. But it is hardly fair to his ghost for his judges to employ such a standard... In this we begin to see the Warren Report not as a judicial finding but as a presentation of a highly responsible prosecutor of the evidence gathered for him by a police force. It is to test such cases that we have an adversary system of justice."

If Mark Lane had signaled the beginning of this era by creating a brief for the defense, the Warren Commission closed this era by issuing a brief for the prosecution. The flaws inherent in this "brief" would be exposed, dramatically, by critics in the coming decade.

the first draft of his autopsy report. Humes was the officer in charge of the formal autopsy after the President's body was flown from Dallas to the Naval hospital in Bethesda, Maryland.

Meagher would find hundreds of other misleading and selective examples both in the Report, and in *The Witnesses*.

"Excerpts from the testimony of Major Eugene D. Anderson and Sergeant James A. Zahm," Meagher would write, "suggest in each case that the shots [Oswald allegedly fired] were not difficult, and that Oswald had the rifle capability to have fired them; however, the Nelson Delgado testmony indicating that Oswald was a poor rifleman is omitted, and

only Delgado's remarks about Oswald's views on capitalism are included, despite many elements in his testimony of far greater importance." [Delgado was a Marine Corps buddy of Oswald.]

"*The Witnesses*," Meagher concluded, "is [thus] one of the most biased offerings ever to masquerade as objective information. In publishing this paperback, *The Times* engaged in uncritical partisanship, the antithesis of responsible journalism."

Sylvia Meagher's voice was, however, alone in the wilderness in the fall of 1964. The American people wanted Lee Harvey Oswald to be the lone assassin. The alternative was simply too dark to contemplate.

BOOK TWO

The Fall of the House of Warren

While the public and the mainstream media seemed pacified by the Warren Commission's conclusions, it wasn't long before independent skeptics started boring holes in the foundation of the Warren Report. Scrutiny of the Report's 26 volumes of testimony revealed to critics a trove of contradictions from which they started to build their counter arguments.

In 1965, Gerald Ford tried to bolster the Lone Gunman theory by publishing the first Oswald biography, *Portrait of an Assassin*. Nowhere in his book, however, did Ford reveal that he had acted as an informant for J. Edgar Hoover while serving as a Warren Commissioner.

In the summer of 1966 the kettle was brought to full boil with publication of Mark Lane's *Rush to Judgment* and Edward Jay Epstein's *Inquest: The Warren Commission and the Establishment of Truth*. Lane concentrated on the crucial evidence left out of the Warren Report, demonstrating that the case *against* Oswald as the lone assassin was as compelling as the case the Report had created.

Epstein's *Inquest* provided a vivid insider's picture of the Commission at work, showing how at every turn, the Commission had been torn by the inherent contradiction between probing for the truth and protecting national security interests. *Inquest* revealed how the Commission had shut down its probe on a number of critical occasions.

As a result of these, and other publications, the public's faith in the Warren Report was badly shaken, and the critics began to search elsewhere for a more convincing explanation of the truth of Dealey Plaza.

11

Arguments on the Left

The I.F. Stone-Bertrand Russell Controversy

While many of the nation's political pundits spent the fall of 1964 assuring the American public that the Warren Report was more or less definitive, an ideological range war broke out between two of the Left's most principled spokesmen, I.F. Stone, writing in his own *I.F. Stone's Weekly*, and Lord Bertrand Russell, writing in the pages of M.S. Arnoni's *A Minority of One*.

The rift would leave the Left divided on the issue of the Kennedy assassination for years to come.

The controversy was initiated by Lord Russell in an article published in the September, 1964 issue of Mr. Arnoni's journal. "The official version of the assassination of President Kennedy," Lord Russell began, "has been so riddled with contradictions that it has been abandoned and rewritten no less than three times.

"Blatant fabrications," Russell continued, "have received very widespread coverage by the mass media, but denials of these same lies have gone unpublished. Photographs, evidence and affidavits have been doctored out of recognition. Some of the most important aspects of the case against Lee Harvey Oswald have been completely blacked out. Meanwhile, the FBI, the police and the Secret Service have tried to silence key witnesses or instruct them what evidence to give. Others involved have disappeared or died in extraordinary circumstances... Because of the high office of its members and the fact of its establishment by President Johnson, the Commission has been widely regarded as a body of holy men appointed to pronouce the Truth. An impartial examination of the composition and conduct of the Commission suggests otherwise."

Lord Russell attacked several Warren commissioners in particular. According to the English mathematician, Richard Russell of Georgia and Hale Boggs of Louisiana were men "whose racist views have brought shame on the United States"; Dulles was CIA; McCloy might just as well have been CIA, and Gerald Ford "was a leader of the Goldwater movement, and an associate of the FBI."

Russell then listed fifteen different open questions concerning the Warren Report, all of which suggested that Oswald was a member of a much broader conspiracy. He also insinuated that a government investigation of what may have been in part a government operation was a bit like asking the proverbial fox to guard the proverbial henhouse.

In conclusion, Lord Russell announced that he was forming a "Who Killed Kennedy Committee" in Great Britain. Members included playwrights John Arden and J.B. Priestly; professors and critics Herbert Read and William Empson; film director Tony Richardson; historian Hugh Trevor-Roper, and Minister of Parliament Michael Foot.

I.F. STONE'S REACTION TO THIS ARTICLE WAS IMMEDIate. On October 5, 1964, Stone devoted almost the entire contents of his popular newsletter to defending the Warren Report, and attacking his former friend and colleague.

"All my adult life as a newspaperman," Stone stated, "I have been fighting in defense of the Left and of sane politics, against conspiracy theories of history, character assassination, guilt by association and demonology. Now I see elements of the Left using these same tactics in the controversy over the Kennedy assassination and the Warren Commission Report.

"I believe the Commission has done a first-rate job, on a level that does our country proud and is worthy of so tragic an event. I regard the case against Lee Harvey Oswald as the lone killer of the President as conclusive...

"It is one thing to analyze discrepancies. It is quite another to write and speak in just that hysterical and defamatory way from which the Left has suffered in the last quarter century or more of political controversy."

Stone spoke next about his colleague, Lord Russell. "He owes it to all of us who have looked to him as a world spokesman of the peace movement, as a great philosopher and humanitarian, to speak more responsibly on this subject. It was not responsible, on the basis of a transatlantic

The Big Game Theory

Writing in the *New York World Telegram* on September 9, 1964, big game hunter and popular author Robert C. Ruark announced that the Warren Commission's reconstruction of the shooting of President Kennedy sounded like so much bush talk to him. "Over 14 years," Ruark stated, "I personally have fired at least two thousand rounds of ammunition at live targets, from elephant to lion to tiger to buffalo to rhino to dik-dik, the littlest of them all... I have read the [Warren Report] scrupulously, several times, and the ballistic end of it makes no sense to me."

Arguments on the Left

phone call from Mark Lane, to attack the report as 'a sorrily incompetent document' which 'covers its authors in shame' without having first read it."

The Englishman's critique was, in fact, based on early notes made by his friend Mark Lane, prior to the release of the Warren Report. Stone took great exception to this: "In its febrile prejudgement, this is on a par with Lord Russell's earlier statement comparing Lane's defense of Oswald with Zola's defense of Dreyfus, and declaring 'There has never been a more subversive, conspiratorial, unpatriotic or endangering course for the security of the United States and the world than the attempt by the U.S. government to hide the murderers of its recent President.' This assumes, instead of proving. It is slander, not controversy."

Both men were, in fact, uncharacteristically off target. Russell, to borrow a phrase from his friend Mark Lane, had indeed rushed to judgment. The majority of Russell's early reservations would be answered the following month with the publication of the actual Warren Report.

But Stone was also guilty of taking the argument to the opposite extreme. In later years, friends of Stone would claim that the journalist was so relieved that the Commission did not blame the assassination on either Moscow or a Cuban conspiracy that he felt compelled to rush to its defense.

The Russell/Stone controversy, however, was to divide the Left into opposing camps—a division which to this very day characterizes left-wing thinking on the assassination.

A MINORITY OF ONE

M.S. Arnoni's *A Minority of One* —like *I.F. Stone's Weekly*, pretty much a one-man operation—has the distinction of being the first American journal of political consequence to open its pages to the possibility of a conspiracy in the death of President Kennedy.

Arnoni himself began to editorialize on the controversy as early as April, 1964. *A Minority of One* soon became home not only to internationally recognized critics such as Mark Lane, Bertrand Russell, and Conor Cruise O'Brien— it also published important early articles by two Philadelphia critics, Vincent Salandria and Harold Feldman, as well as the early writings of Sylvia Meagher, who would become a titan among early Warren Commission critics.

Salandria and Feldman were among the first independent professionals to visit Dallas in order to reconstruct for themselves the truth of the Report. Based on his own analysis of the shots, trajectories and wounds, Salandria may have been the first critic to reject, on the basis of science, both the Single Bullet and Lone Gunman theories.

Feldman concentrated on the testimony of the 121 known witnesses to the assassination, and was the first to point out that while 32 of these witnesses had told the Commission that the shots must have been fired from the Book Depository, 51 witnesses told the Commission that shots had been fired from the Grassy Knoll. (The remaining 38 were uncertain.) As far as actual eyewitness testimony was concerned, Feldman noted, the Commission's conclusions had certainly been based on underwhelming evidence.

Published out of Passaic, New Jersey, *A Minority of One* provided an early forum for what would soon be called "The Philadelphia School" of Warren Report critics. Led by Arnoni, this school would grow to include Feldman; Salandria; *Greater Philadelphia Magazine* editor, Gaeton Fonzi, research expert and scientist Paul Hoch, and a young Haverford College philosophy professor, Josiah Thompson, who following Salandria's leads, would later write one of the classics of JFK assassination literature, *Six Seconds in Dallas*.

The magazine did indeed offer what was still largely a minority point of view. Other leading magazines of the Left, like *The Nation*, would for the better part of the next thirty years continue to take the I.F. Stone position on the assassination controversy.

Mr. Oswald's Biographer

The Gerald Ford Secret Transcript Controversy

12

Hot on the heels of the release of the Warren Report, the first Lee Harvey Oswald biographies began to hit the bookstores. Dr. Renatus Hartogs, a psychiatrist who had evaluated Oswald as a boy of thirteen, published a book called *Two Assassins*. In what could be considered the Oedipal Theory of the JFK assassination, Hartogs theorized that repressed lust for his mother had caused Oswald to kill Kennedy. In *Oswald*, Kerry Thornley painted a fascinating portrait of his former Marine Corps associate, "Ozzie Rabbit," as a serious, if somewhat cranky, well-read intellectual.

The most important Oswald biography of the entire bunch, however, was written by Warren Commissioner and future President, Gerald Ford, then a Republican Congressman from Michigan. On its publication, Ford's *Portrait of the Assassin*—written with the help of his press secretary, John H. Stile—initiated a new wave of assassination controversy.

In substance, the Ford biography amounted to little more than a recycling of the background information on Oswald which could already be found in the Warren Report. But it was Ford's use of that information which created the problem. In the first very chapter of the book, Ford carried the reader into a previously top secret meeting of the Commission, which had taken place on January 22, 1964.

"No sooner had the Commission investigating President Kennedy's assassination assembled its staff and tentatively outlined methods of operation than it was plunged into an astonishing problem," Ford begins.

"On Wednesday, January 22, the members of the Commission were hurriedly called into emergency session by the chairman. Mr. J. Lee Rankin, newly appointed General Counsel for the Commission, had received a telephone call from Texas. The caller was Mr. Waggoner Carr, the Attorney General of Texas. The information was that the FBI had an undercover agent, and that that agent was none other than Lee Harvey Oswald, the alleged assassin of President Kennedy!"

ALTHOUGH GERALD FORD DID NOT NAME NAMES IN HIS book, the source of this rumor was *Houston Post* reporter Alonzo "Lonnie" Hudkins. Hudkin's source was Allan Sweatt, the chief of the criminal division of the Dallas sheriff's office. Sweatt had told Hudkins that, up until the very day he had shot the President, Oswald was being paid two hundred dollars a month by the FBI, and that his FBI Informant number was S-172. He had been on the payroll since sometime in 1962.

Upon learning the news, Ford recounts, the Commissioners realized they had inherited a two-pronged problem. First question: was Oswald an FBI agent? And secondly, as the FBI was chosen as the Commission's sole investigating arm—how could the Commission ask the Bureau to investigate itself in this matter?

Quoting verbatim, but selectively, from the discussion which ensued, Ford describes the debate among the various Commissioners. He also shows that the Commission's desire not to offend Mr. Hoover was a major part of the consideration.

Finally, quoting from the actual transcript, he concludes with the following brave and independent remarks by General Counsel Rankin.

Mr. Rankin: I don't think the country is going be satisfied with a mere statement from, not to use Mr. Hoover's name, but just examine about any intelligence agency, that Oswald wasn't hired, in the light of this kind of an accusation, a rumor. I think the country is going to expect this Commission to try to find out the facts as to how those things are handled to such an extent that this Commission can fairly say, "In our opinion, [Oswald] was or was not an employee of any intelligence agency of the United States."

And so, Ford writes, "It was the consensus of all seven men that the only way to proceed was to conduct extensive

and thorough hearings of as many witnesses as was necessary to exhaust not just this rumor but dozens of other rumors. Where doubts were cast on any United States agency, independent experts would be hired and the investigation conducted in such a way as to avoid reliance on a questioned authority. No matter what the cost in time or money, every facet of the events in Dallas had to be explored."

In writing this, Gerald Ford tripped over his own ambitions and convictions on at least two occasions. First of all, he paid no attention whatsoever to the fact that it was illegal to quote verbatim from top secret government documents.

It was also bad form, of course, to do so to help sell a book.

Far more importantly, it was risky to quote from this document in a deliberately selective and partisan manner, as Ford had done, particularly if there was the chance that the Government might someday declassify this document, and allow its full contents to be known to the American public. And that is exactly what happened. In 1974, in response to the dogged and persistent efforts of Warren Report critic Harold Weisberg, the

government finally declassified the transcript. Weisberg responded by printing it in full, with commentary and appendix, as the fourth volume in his *Whitewash* series.

THE UNEDITED WAGGONER TRANSCRIPT, AS IT IS NOW known, is fascinating reading. In it we are given perhaps the only real glimpse we'll ever have of the Commission at work behind closed doors.

We learn, for example, that the Commission did take quite seriously rumors concerning Oswald's relationship with the FBI. We note that the Commission knew the FBI already had Oswald's name on a list of potentially dangerous Dallas subversives. The Commission had wondered aloud why the FBI did not inform the Secret Service that a Marxist defector was sitting inside one of the buildings along the Presidential motorcade route. Why hadn't the Bureau told the Secret Service to secure the Book Depository? Could it be that the FBI wasn't worried about Oswald, because he was already on their payroll?

We learn that one of the reasons Chief Justice Warren himself was wary of

soliciting testimony from either reporter Hudkins or his source, Dallas police division chief Allan Sweatt, was that the public might learn about this Oswald/FBI rumor. The transcript quotes Justice Warren saying that "Lee [Rankin] thought that if he went down and asked those people to come up here and testify that they might use the fact that we had asked them to testify as the springboard for an article which would blow this thing out into the public domain, and that we might do a disservice in that way."

We also learn that one of the reasons the Commissioners felt they shouldn't bring this matter to the FBI's attention is that Director Hoover would deny it, whether it were true or not. In the transcript, former CIA Director Allen Dulles matter-of-factly states: "I think under any circumstances, Mr. Hoover would say certainly he didn't have anything to do with this fellow."

At another point, Rankin cites still another problem in approaching the FBI on this matter. "Part of our difficulty in regard to it," Rankin frankly admits, "is that they [the FBI] have no problem. They have decided that it is Oswald who committed the assassination, they have decided that no one else was involved, they have decided—"

Senator Russell interupts: "They have tried the case and reached a verdict on every aspect."

To which Hale Boggs responds: "You have put your finger on it."

Finally, after a lengthy discussion—the actual transcript is 121 pages long—the Commissioners attempt to summarize.

Sen. Russell: It seems to me we have two alternatives. One is we can just accept the FBI's report and go and write the report based on their findings and supported by the raw materials they have given us, or else we can go and try to run down some of these collateral rumors that have just not been dealt with directly in this raw material that we have.

Rep. Boggs: I think we must do the latter.

Sen. Russell: So do I.

Chairman: I think there is no question about it.

Sen Russell: Of course the other is much easier.

W HAT, THEN, WAS THE FINAL OUTCOME of this meeting? The next day Attorney Rankin contacted Mr. Hoover directly. As predicted, Hoover vehemently denied that Oswald ever worked for the FBI. Rankin would later ask Special Counsel for the State of Texas, Leon Jaworski (later to be the Watergate special prosecutor)—to look into the matter.

Jaworski wrote back "that there was absolutely nothing to the story," and so the matter was officially dropped.

None of these incidents, however, found their way into Gerald Ford's book. In spite of Ford's statement "that the only way to proceed was to conduct extensive and thorough hearings of as many witnesses as was necessary to exhaust not just this rumor but dozens of others," neither Hudkins nor Sweatt nor anyone else connected with this story was ever called to testify before the Commission.

The contents of the Waggoner Transcript, the way in which the Commission had handled those contents, and Gerald Ford's unique relationship to the Commission, all triggered a series of revelations which would ultimately undermine the final worth and authority of the Warren Report.

Mr. Hoover's INFORMANT

ALTHOUGH LEE HARVEY OSWALD'S RELATIONSHIP TO THE FBI would remain clouded, on January 20, 1978, The *Washington Post* published a story by reporter George Lardner, Jr. stating that Warren Commissioner Gerald Ford had himself been an FBI informant. Through at least the early part of the investigation, Ford had secretly informed the Bureau on the inner workings of the Commission.

Lardner's story was based on the declassification of still another previously secret government document—a memo written by Cartha DeLoach, Hoover's assistant director at the time of the Warren Commission. In it, DeLoach claimed that Ford had approached him, and "indicated he would keep me thoroughly advised as to the activities of the Commission. He stated this would have to be on a confidential basis; however, he thought that it should be done."

According to DeLoach, Ford "also asked if he could call me from time to time and straighten out questions in his mind concerning our investigation. I told him by all means he should do this. He reiterated that our relationship would, of course, remain confidential.

Hoover was aware of this arrangement. His handwritten remark "well-handled" appears on the DeLoach memo.

Ford would later confirm the story in testimony before the House Select Committee on Assassinations. While in his words, "The relationship did not continue during the investigative period of Commission," it began on December 12, 1963, and was still in place during the time of the Waggoner Transcript. So the problem of what to tell Hoover, and what not to tell Hoover, was, it turned out, somewhat moot—considering that the FBI director had an informant of his own sitting in the room.

The Mysterious Back Wound

The FBI Autopsy Report Controversy

**W**ith the publication of Edward Jay Epstein's *Inquest* and Mark Lane's *Rush to Judgment* in the summer of 1966, a taboo of enormous strength was finally broken. For the first time in the pages of the American press, reviews of these two books contained open challenges to the previously unassailable authority of the lone assassin theory. Students of the assassination began to wonder if a theory alternative to the Warren Report was not now in order.

Inquest was the first of the two books to be published, and it was certainly a shocker. Epstein was a Cornell student who wrote the book to satisfy a graduation requirement. He was the first critic to actually interview the Warren Commissioners and their key staff members before coming to his conclusions. His book would forever be the "inside story of the Warren

Commission," a behind-closed-doors look at the course of the full investigation.

While some of the terrain had been trod earlier by other critics, Epstein's account of the Waggoner Transcript, for example, was informed by interviews with special counsel Rankin, as well as with several Commissioners who had attended the secret meeting in January to deal with the business of Lee Harvey Oswald's possible connection to the FBI.

While numerous critics had questioned Oswald's ability as a rifleman, Epstein's account of the FBI and Army tests of the Mannlicher rifle was informed by his access to a confidential memo staff lawyer Wesley Liebeler had prepared for the Commission. In the memo, Liebeler clearly informed his colleagues that their case against Oswald was weak, and needed more work.

Inquest also provided

the reader with the first "insider" account of Arlen Specter's invention of the single bullet theory. Epstein showed that Specter had advanced his theory in obvious contradiction to autopsy information provided to the Commission from both the Secret Service and the FBI.

Epstein spelled out in considerable detail how the Commission came to reject the autopsy report of FBI special agents Francis X. O'Neill, Jr. and James Sibert, who were present at the Bethesda Naval Hospital autopsy of the President's body, and who provided the FBI's official report of the autopsy proceedings.

The Warren Commission would later claim that the first shot entered "the rear of the neck," passed completely through the neck, and exited through the throat enroute to causing three more wounds in Governor Connally. But the FBI's autopsy report, Epstein explained, indicated that the first shot entered "just below the shoulder," penetrated less than finger length into Kennedy's back, and never exited. Lodged in the President's back, the bullet eventually worked loose and fell out, possibly at Parkland Hospital. It should be noted that the doctors at Bethesda had first focused their attention on the fatal head wound. Discovery of an earlier back wound was almost accidental; it occurred only when attendants turned over Kennedy's body.

"During the later stages of this autopsy," O'Neill and Sibert stated in their report, "Dr. Humes located an opening which appeared to be a bullet hole which was below the shoulders and two inches to the right of the middle line of the spinal column.

"This opening was probed by Dr. Humes with the

Bunched Shirts and Bullet Holes

PUBLICATION OF EDWARD Epstein's *Inquest* thrust staff attorney Arlen Specter into the public spotlight. At the Commission, Specter had been in charge of making sense of the basic facts of the assassination. He would now be called on to defend his contribution to the Report.

It was Specter, the reader will recall, who first asserted that the President's shoulder wound was a transit wound, and that the same bullet had also wounded Governor Connally. In advancing this interpretation, Specter relied on the official autopsy provided by Commander Humes. On the night of the autopsy, however, Humes had located the first shot to hit the President as being in the shoulder, not the neck. But during the following days Humes revised his

original estimation a few inches upward, to formally conclude that the bullet had in fact passed through the President's neck, and had not lodged in the President's back. Specter used Humes' formal report to create the link he needed for his Single Bullet theory, even though a good deal of evidence indicated otherwise.

First of all, the Commission had before it the sketch of the President's body which Humes' associate, Dr. Boswell, had drawn during the autopsy. The sketch has survived, and clearly indicates that Boswell had first located the wound in the shoulder area—consistent with the O'Neill-Sibert report.

Secondly, the FBI took photographs of the President's body, and his clothes, on the night of the autopsy. Although most of these

pictures remained under wraps out of courtesy to the Kennedy family, two photographs do survive from that occasion—one of the back of the President's jacket, the other of the shirt he was wearing (*see following page*).

The bulletholes in the photos certainly seem to indicate an entry wound in the shoulder area.

How could a bullet entering the President's body on a downward trajectory miraculously change course while inside the President, and exit through his neck? Specter would later claim that the shirt and jacket had bunched up as the President was turning to wave to spectators in Dealey Plaza.

Such bunching is not visible, however, in the various films and snapshots taken at the time of the assassination.

finger, at which time it was determined that the trajectory of the missile entering at this point had entered at a downward position of 45 to 60 degrees. Further probing determined that the distance travelled by this missile was a short distance inasmuch as the end of the opening could be felt with the finger."

The O'Neill and Sibert report also presented, albeit in torturous prose, a possible origin for Commission Exhibit 399—the famous "magic" bullet which the Commission would claim passed through both Kennedy and Connally, before ending up, more or less intact, on a stretcher at Parkland Hospital.

"Inasmuch as no complete bullet of any size could be located in the brain area and likewise no bullet could be located in the back or any other area of the body as determined by total body X-rays and inspection revealing there was no point of exit, the individuals were at a loss to explain why they could find no bullets.

"A call was made by Bureau agents to the Firearms Section of the FBI Laboratory, at which time Special Agent Charles L. Killion advised that the Laboratory had received through Secret Service Agent Richard Johnson a bullet which had reportedly been found on a stretcher in the emergency room of Parkland Hospital, Dallas Texas.... Immediately following receipt of this information, this was made available to Dr. Humes who advised that in his opinion this accounted for no bullet being located which had entered [the back, upon first examining the wound]."

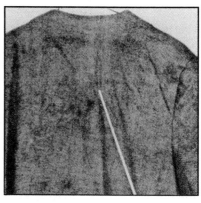

The jacket photograph—Commission Exhibit 59—clearly shows a bullet hole in the back of Kennedy's jacket some 5 3/8" below the top of the collar.

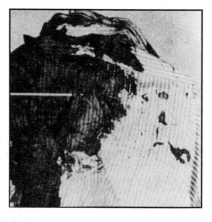

The photograph of the President's shirt—Commission Exhibit 60—presumably shows a hole from the same bullet some 5 3/4" below the collar.

NOT PUBLISHED ANYWHERE IN THE WARREN Report's twenty-six volumes, the O'Neill-Sibert report was clearly a document of utmost importance, especially considering that it was supported by other eyewitnesses present at the autopsy.

"[In addition to both FBI agents], two Secret Service agents—Roy Kellerman and William Geer—were present at President Kennedy's autopsy," Epstein writes. "Agent Roy Kellerman testified: 'There were three gentlemen who performed this autopsy. A Colonel Finck—during the examination of the President, from the hole that was in his shoulder, and with a probe, and we were standing right

alongside of him, he is probing inside the shoulder with his instrument and I said 'Colonel, where did it go?' He said, 'There are no lanes from an outlet of this entry in this man's shoulder.' Agent William Greer also testified that the autopsy doctors could not find a path for the bullet."

The O'Neill-Sibert report thus flatly contradicted the official version of the autopsy which would eventually be found in the Warren Report. It cannot, however, be found among all the other Warren Commission public documents. Agents O'Neill and Sibert were never called to testify before the Warren Commission.

14 Implicit Instructions

The Warren Commission National Security Controversy

Publication of Edward Jay Epstein's *Inquest* marked an important turning point in the study of the assassination of John Fitzgerald Kennedy. By choosing to ignore the implications of a good deal of the evidence it had on hand, the Warren Report would eventually earn more renown for the case it chose not to prosecute, than for the case it would make against dead and defenseless Lee Harvey Oswald.

Why had the Commission remained so insistent that Lee Harvey Oswald alone had killed John F. Kennedy? Why had the Commission been so persistently skeptical and dismissive with evidence that seemed to vary from the seemingly pre-ordained Lone Gunman conclusion? In these matters, *Inquest* offered a compelling account of what had been wrong with the Warren Commission right from the start.

For Epstein, the problem was inherent in the dual nature of the mandate given to the Commission. From the beginning, the Commission was charged with arriving at the full truth of the Kennedy assassination without revealing important details concerning our "national security."

BUT HOW COULD ANYONE UNDERSTAND THE REAL nature of Oswald, for example, without also understanding his unique relationship not just with the FBI, but also with the CIA, the Office of Naval Intelligence, US Army Intelligence, the State Department, and the Intelligence Services of at least two foreign nations, the USSR and Cuba?

How could anyone really understand Jack Ruby without fully investigating his links to a network of mob bosses who only a few years earlier had stretched their gambling empire from the deserts of Nevada to the faro tables of Batista's Havana?

As the Warren Commission quickly realized, a full examination of either Oswald or Ruby was fraught with serious national security implications.

Ultimately the Commission had to decide which was more important: protecting national security interests by keeping the existence of certain covert, criminal-infested networks a secret; or openly investigating a web of secret associations which surrounded the lives and deeds of the two key players in the death of John F. Kennedy.

This would neither be the first, nor the last time an official U.S. government investigation would be faced with this kind of dilemma. This quandary would appear continuously throughout the course of the next few decades, from Warren to Watergate to Iran-Contra.

"THE PURPOSE OF THE Warren Commission," Epstein writes, "was never fully stated in its Report." The executive order which created the Commission listed its "purposes" as examining evidence, conducting further investigations, evaluating facts and circumstances, and reporting the findings to the President. There was, Epstein showed, an important distinction between the fact-finding function of the Commission, and its ultimate purpose.

"... The circumstances surrounding the Chief Justice's appointment to the Commission suggests [this ultimate] purpose," writes Epstein. "Anthony Lewis, then the *New York Times* Supreme Court correspondent, reported that when Warren was first asked to serve on the Commission 'he flatly said no.' President Johnson then called Warren to the White House and spoke to him 'about patriotism, about the new President's urgent need to settle the assassination rumors, about the special trust people in foreign lands would have in an investigation over which he presided'....

[This account implies] that one purpose of the Commission was to protect the national interest by settling 'assassination rumors' and restoring American prestige abroad.

"Other members of the Commission also conceived of the Commission's purpose in terms of the national interest. Allen Dulles said that an atmosphere of rumor and suspicion interferes with the functioning of the government, especially abroad, and one of the main tasks of the Commission was to dispel rumors. Congressman Gerald Ford said that dispelling damaging rumors was a major concern of the Commission, and most members of the Commission agreed.

"There was thus a dualism in purpose. If the explicit purpose of the Commission was to ascertain and expose the facts, the implicit purpose was to protect the national interest by dispelling rumors. These two purposes were compatible so long as the damaging rumors were untrue. But what if a rumor damaging to the national interest proved to be true? The Commission's explicit purpose would dictate that the information be exposed regardless of the consequences, while the Commission's implicit purpose would dictate that the rumor be dispelled regardless of the fact that it was true.

"In a conflict of this sort," Epstein concludes, "one of the Commission's purposes would emerge as dominant."

The Real McCloy

When it came to National Security—and expanding the interests of American business abroad—few men were as dedicated as former Chase Manhattan Bank chairman John J. McCloy. As High Commissioner in Germany after WWII, McCloy watched West German Intelligence take form under the leadership of former Nazi general Reinhard Gehlen. McCloy would later say that the job of the Warren Commission was to "show the world that the U.S. was not a banana republic where a government could be changed by conspiracy." He spoke from experience: after the CIA toppled the Figueres government in Costa Rica in 1956, McCloy became a director of the United Fruit Company—with the CIA, the architect of one of the most famous "banana republics" in all of Central America.

No member of the Commission was more sensitive to national security implications than Allen Dulles. He had been one of the architects of the National Security Act of 1947—the act which gave birth to an invisible government of intelligence operations which came to dominate the secret history of the Cold War.

The network brought into being by the National Security Act began with the CIA, but was extended to also include the National Security Council, the Defense Intelligence · Agency, the National Security Agency, Army Intelligence, Navy Intelligence, Air Force Intelligence, the State Department's Bureau of Intelligence and Research, the Atomic Energy Commission, and—last but not least—Mr. Hoover's Federal Bureau of Investigation.

This new spook bureaucracy required a new kind of spook bureaucrat to swim smoothly in its streams. Well-bred, discreet, and a member of one of Wall Street's most powerful families, Allen Dulles certainly fit the bill. He had been a bureau chief in the Office of Strategic Services in Germany during World War II. Eisenhower appointed Dulles to be his CIA Director in the spring of 1953.

At CIA, Dulles had been the point man for intelligence operations which helped install the Shah of Iran in 1953; helped destabilize the Arbenz government in Guatemala in 1954, the Nasser government in Egypt in 1956, and helped in the 1956 elimination of the Figueres administration in Costa Rica. Dulles also presided over a series of chess moves in Southeast Asia which escalated into the war in Vietnam by the end of this era.

Allen Dulles had one other impor-

tant feather in his cap. Unknown to his fellow Warren Commissioners, Dulles had created a full-fledged assassination bureau inside the Agency by the dawn of the 1960s. Having given up on trying to "invent" assassins through mind control and drug- related conditioning programs, Dulles had turned to the Mob for help in launching assas-

sination missions in South Vietnam against Diem, in the Congo against Lumumba, and against Castro in Cuba.

In 1960, Dulles had taken out a contract on Castro's life with a triumvirate of highly-placed Mafiosi—mob boss Johnny Rosselli, Chicago Mayor Richard Daley's associate Sam Giancana, and the former Cuban gambling overlord Santos Trafficante. Few people wanted Castro out of power more than Trafficante. He and his associates lived for the day when wide open Mob-controlled vice could be returned to Havana.

Early in his administration the late President supported many of Dulles' clandestine operations. But their relationship ended in bitterness when Kennedy fired Dulles from the CIA. JFK felt that Dulles' high-handed oversight of the infamous Bay of Pigs invasion amounted to betrayal, since it put Kennedy in an unwinnable situation. As a result, Kennedy had vowed to "break the CIA into a thousand pieces and scatter it to the winds."

But by 1964, Kennedy was dead. The CIA, however, was still very much in business. And Allen Dulles, the "Invisible Emperor," was back minding the store as a member of the Warren Commission.

Voices from the Grassy Knoll

The Mark Lane "Second Assassin" Controversy

**M**ark Lane's *Rush to Judgment* was released three months after the publication of Edward Jay Epstein's *Inquest. Rush to Judgment* would soon become the most popular critical repudiation of the Warren Commission's version of who killed JFK. While Epstein had diligently tried to create an objective and impartial study of how the Commission arrived at its verdict, Lane felt no such compulsion. His book was a legal brief for a dead defendent, Lee Harvey Oswald. Marguerite Oswald, the alleged assassin's mother, had, in fact, hired Lane to represent her son. In his appearances before the Warren Commission, Lane had earned the panel's undying contempt by acting the part of Oswald's attorney.

Lane enjoyed the spotlight. In the fall of 1966, he could be found making his way from talk shows—satirist and political talk show host Mort Sahl was one enthusiastic supporter—to college campuses, lecturing and debating with any and all who rose to challenge his views on the sinister forces behind the death of JFK.

Edward Jay Epstein, by comparison, seemed a mere babe in the woods. Very much the young journalist, pleased to have cultivated a slew of official government contacts for his budding journalism career, Epstein didn't have the stomach for accusations. In the end, he felt the Commission's error was

almost theoretical, perhaps even gentlemanly, in nature. The error—it if was an error—was to uphold the national security interest at the expense of a full investigation of conspiracy rumors and allegations.

As Epstein argued the point, some might even find a measure of patriotism in the job the Commission had done.

Mark Lane, on the other hand, suspected the worst. The word *coverup* came far more easily to his tongue than did the word *oversight*. With the arrival of his book, a certain all-knowing conspiratorial tone—first adopted by the European critics—became firmly entrenched in the minds of many of the people who would come to study JFK assassination literature and lore.

"Why, this is sheer demonology," some of Lane's most strident critics claimed.

And it was.

From this point forward, one of the tests for future students of the assassination would be: Can you bring yourself to believe that evil men often become national leaders, and then regularly lie to the public to hide the true nature of their crimes?

In these pre-Watergate days, most Americans could not.

Those who could, however, found a prophet in Mark Lane—and a bible in *Rush to Judgment*.

It certainly did not hurt Lane, or the sales of his book, that one of his first reviewers was novelist Norman Mailer, himself no stranger to the forces of darkness which occasionally steal sunlight from the planet.

"Lane presents a thousand items of clear-cut doubt in 400 pages, material sufficient for five years of real investigation by any fair country commission," Mailer wrote of *Rush to Judgment*. "Three cheers for Mark Lane. His work is not without a trace of that stature we call heroic."

S.M. "Skinny" Holland

Carolyn Walther

Amos Euins, Jr.

Re-reading *Rush to Judgment* today, what does in fact seem heroic is the sheer chutzpah of this urban lawyer, a long way from his native Brooklyn, arriving in the middle of Texas to conduct his own private counter-investigation, by interviewing for himself the critical eyewitnesses—both those who testified, and those who were not called to testify. In retrospect, these eyewitnesses stand out as the real heroes of *Rush to Judgment*.

By most accounts, there had been 121 eyewitnesses to the assassination of President Kennedy. The clear majority felt shots had come from the rear of the grassy knoll. If it had been an election, the grassy knoll ticket would have been considered the winner in a landslide.

Could all of these people have been mistaken? It was possible, but it sure wasn't likely. A savvy trial lawyer, Mark Lane let his final case stand on the word—and the character—of grassy knoll witnesses whose testimony had largely been ignored by the Warren Commission.

In the pages of his book—and later in the film Lane created with the late Emil de Antonio—we meet for the first time certain eyewitnesses—Sam Holland, Carolyn Walther, Amos Euins, and others—not likely to have been mistaken as to the location of at least some of the shots which killed John Kennedy.

Lane thus became the first critic to systematically develop a theory of the Kennedy assassination alternative to the Lone Gunman. For this contribution alone, the combative lawyer from Brooklyn earned his own unique place in American history.

The grassy knoll eye-witnesses were a varied and intelligent group of people. Mary Woodward, a reporter for *The Dallas Morning News*, witnessed the shooting from the sidewalk on Elm Street, at the foot of the knoll, in front and directly to the left of the picket fence which may have hidden a second gunman.

Woodward told authorities that as the President approached, "suddenly there was a horrible, ear-shattering noise coming from behind us, and [from] a little to the right." Abraham Zapruder, clutching his movie camera, was stand-ing on the pergola in the back of the knoll directly behind Wood-ward. He also maintained the shots came from behind him.

Four Dallas policemen rushed up the knoll upon first hearing rifle fire. Dallas Deputy Constable Seymour Weitzman was among the first to reach the area. He asked a yardman where the shots had come from and the man pointed to the shrubbed area next to the fence. Dallas patrolman J.M.

Smith followed Weitzman into the area, and reported that he "caught the smell of gunpowder there."

Seven Dallas Union Terminal railroadmen witnessed the shooting of the President from the overpass, and immediately ob-served a puff of smoke rising from the fence area. Two of the men, S.M. Holland and James L. Simmons, ran from the overpass and into the yard behind the fence. They found footprints behind the

Lee Bowers

fence, and mud on the back bum-per of a car which the gunman, or his spotter, could have stood on.

The witness with the best view of this area was Lee Bowers, a Union Terminal switchman, who was sitting in a fourteen-foot tower overlooking the fence area and the parking lot which bordered it. In his tes-timony to the Warren Com-mission, Bowers recalled that the area had been sealed off by police at about 10 a.m. At about 12:10 p.m. the first of three cars made a drive-by of the yard, learning that the area was a dead end, with only a single entry point.

Bowers detailed that two of the cars were out-of-state; both were caked in mud; both featured "Goldwater for President" stickers on the rear bumper. One of the drivers seemed to be talking through a remote telephone as he probed the area, Bowers noted.

Several minutes later, Bowers caught sight of the Presidential motorcade as it turned down Elm. He also noticed two men standing at the fence about 15 feet apart, as the motorcade approached.

Then shots rang out. "There was a flash of light or something [in the fence area]," Bowers testified. "Something I could not identify... some unusual occurrence—a flash of light or s m o k e o r something which caused me to feel that something out of the ordinary had occurred there."

At this point in his testimony, the Commission investigator diverted questioning away from the grassy knoll, and Bowers' official recollections went no further.

For skeptics, the knoll was now ground zero. The second assassin scenario would eventually become as important to conspiracy theorists as the sixth floor of the Book Depository was for the Warren Commission.

Foundations of Doubt

The Inquest-Rush to Judgment Controversy

By the fall of 1966 the collective impact of *Inquest* and *Rush to Judgment* prompted a major review in even the most established press circles as to the true value of the Warren Report.

"The Warren Report is not an edifice to crumble overnight if at all," the editors of the dignified (London) *Sunday Times* stated in a special supplement published on August 21, 1996. "It is buttressed by some most solid reputations in the United States, including that of its chairman, Chief Justice Earl Warren. And, understandably, it is not something that Americans want to see crumble. The Warren finding that it was a lone nut who killed the President provided certainty—and a welcome certainty—after a period of frequently wild rumour-mongering. If the critics have their way, the whole situation must be plunged back into a state of flux.

"Slowly, inexorably, this seems to be coming about. The Commission has been subject to a storm of assaults; but in essence it is two painstakingly cool-toned books which have undermined the foundations. These are *Rush to Judgment* by the New York lawyer, Mark Lane, and *Inquest*, by political scientist, Edward Jay Epstein."

In fact, Epstein and Lane owed a debt of gratitude to two lesser-known critics, Vincent Salandria and Harold Weisberg.

With his insider's access to the Commission, Epstein was able to go one step further, showing the difficulty, and the skepticism, which faced Arlen Specter when he attempted to construct his controversial theory. Yet in an article in the magazine *Liberation* in January of 1965, it was Salandria who first drew attention to the improbabilities inherent in the single bullet theory.

In a follow-up article in the March 1965 issue of *Liberation*, Salandria also was the first to indicate the differences between the initial FBI report and the official autopsy. Salandria was also the first to wonder aloud why the Commission had not immediately called for all relevant x-rays and photographs. Why had they chosen instead to rely on Dr. Boswell's contradictory pencil sketches? Although Epstein later took the question further by investigating the controversy through personal interviews with the Commission and its staff, it was Salandria who first opened this trail.

Similarly, many of the questions raised in Mark Lane's *Rush to Judgment* had been asked one year earlier by Harold Weisberg, a private citizen and former Senate investigator, in the first of a series of self-printed typewritten books called *Whitewash*.

Weisberg would prove relentless—and, on occasion, successful—in his demands for additional documents, memos, and photographs collected by the Commission but not released to the general public. Weisberg was among the first critics to suggest the possibility of a Lee Harvey Oswald double, as a good deal of classified testimony found Oswald in two places at once. The double, Weisberg intimated, may have been used to set up the real Oswald as the patsy for the crime.

Based on photographic evidence which he had gathered, Weisberg was also the first to theorize that the Dal-Tex building—on the opposite corner of Elm and Houston from the Book Depository—may have been the site of a second, or even third, assassin. The bullet which entered Kennedy's back on an eleven degree upward trajectory, he maintained, certainly couldn't have been fired from a sixth floor elevation.

WHAT DISTINGUISHED EACH OF THESE CRITICS was a matter of temperament and critical style. Epstein took a scalpel to the Warren Report. Salandria, more forcefully, preferred a crowbar. Weisberg attacked with a machete, while the combative Lane was satisfied with nothing less than a Gatling gun.

Whatever their contrasting aesthetics, by the fall of 1966 popular opinion was swinging away from the Warren Commission, and beginning to come the way of this odd and unlikely group of very persistent critics.

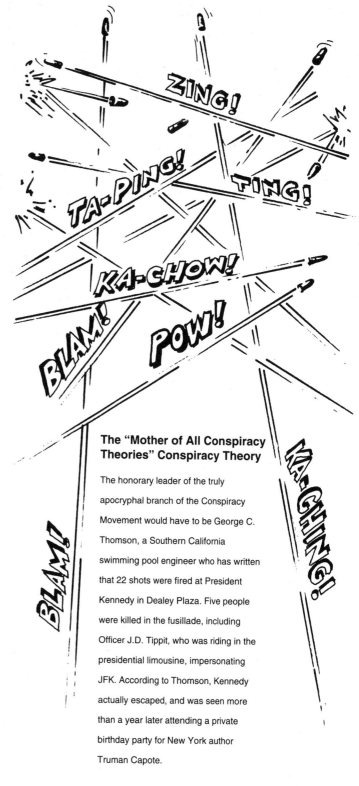

The "Mother of All Conspiracy Theories" Conspiracy Theory

The honorary leader of the truly apocryphal branch of the Conspiracy Movement would have to be George C. Thomson, a Southern California swimming pool engineer who has written that 22 shots were fired at President Kennedy in Dealey Plaza. Five people were killed in the fusillade, including Officer J.D. Tippit, who was riding in the presidential limousine, impersonating JFK. According to Thomson, Kennedy actually escaped, and was seen more than a year later attending a private birthday party for New York author Truman Capote.

THE THIRD INNING STRETCH

The controversy surrounding the death of President Kennedy had now entered the third major phase of the debate. Initially only Mark Lane and a group of European critics had challenged the official response to the killing. With the publication of the Warren Report, the early dissenters were drowned out, as one major news agency after another praised the Commission for its work. Now, with the first serious attacks on the Commission in print, the debate began to edge back toward those who smelled a conspiracy.

A special *Insight* supplement published in the *Sunday Times* listed at least five major open questions.

• **Was Oswald a capable enough marksman?** If the FBI and the Secret Service had failed, the *Times* asked, how could a mediocre rifleman like Lee Harvey Oswald have made such spectacularly effective shots, particularly with a misaligned scope?

• **Was the trajectory of the Single Bullet possible?** While only a single bullet theory would fit the evidence the Commission had cited, there remained a problem of trajectory. As Salandria and Epstein had pointed out, it would take a magic bullet to be able to travel the route required to wound both Kennedy and Connally.

• **How many bullets were actually fired?** The Commission claimed only three. Yet, if the FBI autopsy report was accurate, one bullet had hit the President in the back without transiting. A second bullet then hit the Governor—a bullet which could not have been fired by the Mannlicher-Carcano, if indeed the Mannlicher had fired the first shot. There simply wasn't enough of an interval between the two shots. A third bullet apparently missed the limousine entirely, striking against the curb, then grazing a bystander more than 150 feet down Elm near the underpass. The fatal shot was then fired—*or was it two shots?*—blowing the President's brain out of his head.

• **What about a second shooter?** The physical evidence implied the presence of a second—possibly, even a third—shooter, and this conclusion was reinforced by eyewitness testimony. As Mark Lane ably noted, the majority of the eyewitnesses thought that at least one of the shots had been fired from the fence area at the rear of the grassy knoll.

Many of the remaining eyewitnesses testified that they heard shots from the "vicinity" of the Book Depository—but as Harold Weisberg pointed out, that "vicinity" could also include the Dal-Tex building.

• **Had the Commission blundered?** *The Times* suggested that somewhere in the sheer confusion of the evidence, the Warren Commission had lost its moorings. As both Weisberg and Lane never failed to mention, the Commission had heard contradictory testimony on almost every major aspect of the case. In the end, however, it had chosen to promote only that evidence which supported a Lone Gunman.

The Agency Exerts Its Influence

The CIA Counter Attack Controversy

The Central Intelligence Agency was, by the spring of 1967, clearly worried about the mounting anti-Warren Commission sentiment. The Agency's concerns were revealed in a now-declassified internal memo distributed to station chiefs on April Fool's Day, 1967.

"In most cases the critics have speculated as to the existence of some kind of conspiracy," the memo states, "and often they have implied that the Commission itself was involved. Presumably as a result of the increasing challenge to the Warren Commission's report, a public opinion poll recently indicated that 46% of the American public did not think that Oswald acted alone, while more than half of those polled thought that the Commission had left some questions unresolved. Doubtless polls abroad would show similar, or possibly more adverse, results.

"This trend of opinion is a matter of concern to the U.S. government, including our organization. The members of the Warren Commission were naturally chosen for their integrity, experience, and prominence. They represented both major parties, and they and their staff were deliberately drawn from all sections of the country. Just because of the standing of the Commissioners, efforts to impugn their rectitude and wisdom tend to cast doubt on the whole leadership of American society. Moreover, there seems to be an increasing tendency to hint that President Johnson himself, as the one person who might be said to have benefited, was in some way responsible for the assassination.

"Innuendo of such seriousness affects not only the individuals concerned but also the whole reputation of the American government. Our organization itself is directly involved: among other facts, we contributed information to the investigation. Conspiracy theories have frequently thrown suspicion on our organization, for example by falsely alleging that Lee Harvey Oswald worked for us. The aim of this dispatch is to provide material for countering and

The Division Five & Aristotle Onassis Conspiracy Theories

However justifiable, the CIA's paranoia was more than matched by two of the largest field theories concerning the Kennedy Assassination. In *Nomenclature of an Assassination Cabal*, William Torbitt maintains that the murder was executed by Division Five of the FBI, acting on behalf of a vast conspiracy including Czarist Russians; the American Council of Churches; various Cuban exile groups; a Texas crime syndicate; and the Security Division of NASA, under the direction of rocket scientist Wernher von Braun. In *The Gemstone Files*, the unsigned author—alleged to be an American named Bruce Roberts—pins the crime on Greek shipping magnate Aristotle Onassis. According to the author, Jacqueline Kennedy was sailing with Onassis aboard the Cristina when, on November 1, 1963, JFK first got wind of the plot against him. The President called the Cristina immediately, and is alleged to have told his wife—"Get off that yacht [even] if you have to swim."

discrediting the claims of the conspiracy theorists, so as to inhibit the circulation of such claims in other countries. Background information is supplied in a classified section and in a number of unclassified documents."

As part of its counterattack, the CIA decided, not for the first time, to involve itself in the book reviewing business. To influence opinion in media outlets where the debate was already underway, the Agency recommended "discussing the publicity problem with liaison and friendly elite contacts (especially politicians and editors)." Talking discreetly with these contacts, agents were instructed to point out "that parts of the conspiracy talk appear to be deliberately generated by Communist propaganda."

Agents were also urged "to employ propaganda assets to answer and refute the attack of the critics. Book reviews and feature articles," the Memo states, "are particularly appropriate for this purpose."

For more generalized media discussions, agents were given a kind of top ten list of compatible party lines they were to sell.

The Agency added two attachments to the memo. One was devoted to a background survey of all recent works attacking the Report. In this attachment, the question of Communist sympathies was again stressed to the CIA station chiefs. Agents were urged to remind their contacts and assets that some of the critics "appear to have been predisposed by anti-American, far-left, or Communist sympathies."

German writer Joachim Joesten, for example, was once a member of the Communist Party, the memo stated. The Agency based its assertion on Gestapo World War II documents now part of its voluminous archives. Joesten's American publisher, Carl Marzani, "was sentenced to jail by a federal jury for once concealing his Communist Party membership," the Agency claimed.

Mark Lane also had to be watched closely. As the attachment indicated, Lane had "attended the 8th Congress of the International Association of Democractic Lawyers (an international Communist front organization) in Budapest from 31 March to 5 April 1964, where he expounded his (pre-Report) views on the assassination."

These would be good issues for our friends to raise, the Agency suggested, in future articles and reviews to be planted in the popular press.

A Magic Bullet...

Had he known of its existence at the time, Edward Jay Epstein might have taken comfort in the knowledge that his book, *Inquest*, rated an attachment all its own in the Central Intelligence Agency's counter-strategy memo. The Agency clearly feared his attack on the Warren Report more than most.

In the attachment, the Agency offers its troops two points of attack for disparaging Epstein's work. First, station chiefs were reminded that FBI agents Sibert and O'Neill were simply not informed that the first bullet had entered Kennedy in the back of the neck, and not in the shoulder area as they originally detailed in their autopsy report. Secondly, station chiefs were told that, in spite of photographic evidence to the contrary, they should simply ignore the coat and shirt evidence that seemed to support a bullet hole in JFK's back. The President was waving at the time he

was shot, the CIA reasoned, and his coat and shirt had risen up his back accordingly. Finally, the Agency reminded its chiefs that the autopsy sketch locating the President's wound in the upper back was drawn in haste by Dr. Boswell. Later, upon questioning, Boswell corrected his recollection of the wounds, making it compatible with the neck transit theory.

The Agency also made a considerable effort to provide its chiefs with a rather imaginative response to Epstein's criticism of the Single Bullet theory. "While not likely," the attachment states, "it was *possible* [italicized in the original] that President Kennedy could have been hit more than 2.3 seconds before Connally.

"As Arlen Specter, a Commission attorney and a principal adherent of the 'one-bullet theory' says, 'the Zapruder film is two-dimensional and one cannot say exactly when Connally, let alone the President, was hit...'

"The 'earliest possible time' used by Epstein [for the hit] is based on the belief that, for an interval before

that time, the view of the car from the Book Depository window was probably blocked by the foliage of an oak tree.

...In the words of the Commission's Report, 'it is unlikely that the assassin would deliberately have shot with a view obstructed by the oak tree when he was about to have a clear opportunity."

Yes, the Agency states, it was "*unlikely* [italicized in original] but not impossible."

As for Governor Connally's testimony that he was not hit by the same bullet that hit JFK, the chiefs were reminded that the Governor "did not testify that he saw the President hit before he was hit himself; he testifed that he heard a first shot and started to turn to see what had happened."

Besides, the Agency concludes, "the Commission did not pretend that the two men could not possibly have been hit separately." Oswald could, after all, have gotten off his successful first shot, be it in the back or neck, while the President was hidden from his view in the foliage of what now became a magical oak tree.

...or a Magic Tree?

The Walter, Dan and Eric Show

The CBS Report Controversy

Whatever the influence of the CIA's proposed attack on the critics, the year 1967 did belong to the defenders of the Warren Report. That year Charles Roberts's *The Truth about the Assassination*, with an introduction by JFK's former press secretary, Pierre Salinger, was published by Grosset & Dunlap. A former White House correspondent for *Newsweek*, Roberts basically quoted the Warren Report back to the critics in his brief but incisive book.

The Scavengers and Critics of the Warren Report by Richard Warren Lewis, was published the same year by Dell paperbacks. Lewis based his book on interviews with the critics conducted by Lawrence Schiller for one of the first record albums on the assassination, *The Controversy*. Lewis's *Scavengers* was by far the nastier, more gossipy, and more interesting book. Lewis depicted Lane as a political opportunist, Epstein as a

smartass young punk, and Harold Weisberg as an old-fashioned American crackpot.

Neither book, however, buttressed the official explanations already found in the Warren Report. It would take the combined might of Walter Cronkite, Dan Rather, and the full weight of the Columbia Broadcasting System, to launch the year's most important critical counterattack.

STARTING ON JUNE 25, 1967, AND running for four consecutive nights, the network broadcast "CBS News Inquiry: The Warren Report," hosted by Walter Cronkite and featuring Dan Rather reporting directly from the sixth floor of the Texas School Book Depository, with Eric Sevareid offering final commentary.

During the course of these four nights, only once did CBS go beyond the

Warren Report. This occurred, predictably enough, with regard to the now-infamous Single Bullet. At the end of the first night's broadcast, Cronkite announced: "We have made three additions to the account given in the Warren Report, each of which rests on evidence at least as persuasive as any provided by the Commission.

"Our analysis of the Zapruder film suggests strongly the first shot was fired at frame 186. We have shown that the Zapruder camera was quite possibly running slower than the Commission thought. The earlier shot and the slow camera together mean that the rifleman may have had additional time to get off three shots. We have shown by carefully controlled experiments that a Mannlicher-Carcano rifle can be fired more rapidly and accurately than the Commission believed.

"Now these points strenghten the Warren Report's basic finding. They significantly weaken a central contention of the critics—their contention that Oswald could not have done it because he did not have enough time to fire. It is now reasonable to assume that the first shot fired through a tree missed its mark, and that it was this shot that Governor Connally heard. The Governor's insisted all along that he was not struck by the first shot. It now appears that he was correct."

Under scrutiny, however, the network's contribution to the case was babble. First of all, no one doubted that Oswald's Mannlicher-Carcano could be fired fast enough to get off three rounds in less than five seconds. The problem was never the total elapsed time of the shooting. The problem was the interval of time between each shot.

And here is where CBS made its most important leap: what if the assassin had fired the first shot a micro-second or two earlier than the Warren Commission had allowed? What if Oswald had first fired at Frame 186 of the Zapruder film—that brief micro-second when the President would have been visible to a sixth floor assassin through the foliage of the old oak tree?

While this new scenario would allow enough time, it was, in the end, less persuasive then the theory first advanced by the Warren Commission. In the new scenario—apart from making Oswald's marksmanship even more miraculous—the second shot would still had to have followed a fantastic trajectory. Moreover, as the

What's the Frequency, Dan?

Dan Rather secured a place in assassination lore for being the first journalist to view the Zapruder film. Unfortunately, he reported to millions of people on Nov. 23, 1963 that the film showed JFK's head lurching forward slightly upon impact. He neglected to mention that the President's head then explodes in a violent backward motion. This omission fueled coverup stories for years to come. In his autobiography, Rather states proudly that his technique for news gathering is to "watch and listen as closely as I possibly can, trying to *burn* it into my head, so that if I have to describe a scene again and again I can." In the same tome, Rather says of the Zapruder snafu, "I challenge anyone to watch for the first time a 22-second film of devastating impact, run several blocks, then describe what they have seen in its entirety, without notes."

third shot would have to remain the fatal head shot, you still had to account for a fourth shot which had hit the curb and wounded bystander James Tague, almost two hundred feet down Elm, at the foot of the Underpass.

Some Americans were no doubt reassured by the fatherly Walter Cronkite of the Warren Report's veracity. But to hardcore researchers, the CBS report added only more confusion and doubt to an open-ended murder case growing more baffling all the time. Back in April, the CIA had thought that the Oak Tree Shot scenario might be a good way to counter the critics. Three months later this strange and simple-minded argument would now be employed by CBS as the cornerstone of the network's defense of the Warren Report.

The Company Wishes You a Happy New Year

In 1953, after being appointed to the position of Director of the Central Intelligence Agency, one of the first programs that future Warren Commissioner Allen Dulles put into motion was the recruitment of American journalists to help in the overall information gathering mission of the Agency. At the peak of its recruitment efforts in the 1950s, the Agency could list some 400 working journalists as assets to the Company.

No news organization in the world ever worked more closely with the Agency on these efforts than did CBS under the leadership of board chairman William Paley. Only *Life* magazine, under the direction of C.D. Jackson, a former White House aide and national security "specialist," would rival CBS in terms of an ongoing relationship with the CIA.

CBS foreign correspondents were regularly debriefed by the Agency upon returning from overseas assignments; the CBS film, photo and research archives were always at the disposal of the Company. At one point CBS even allowed CIA agents to occupy the network's press booth at the United Nations. From that vantage point CIA specialists were able to better lip-read conversations within the Soviet delegation.

The relationship between the Agency and the Network would remain comfortable into the 1970s. During this interim period, CIA Director Allen Dulles would host a party for CBS each New Year's Day. According to former CIA analyst William Bundy "Allen would get them [the CBS people] to a dinner at the Alibi Club in Washington, a favorite place of his, and it would be a terribly nice party. There would be about twenty-five of us all told, about fifteen of them from CBS. We had a CIA man next to each CBS man, and there was general table conversation, very useful in giving the feeling of Allen's thinking without giving them secret material, and

at the same time extracting their views and thoughts—he [Dulles] was particularly good at this. Later, critics like David Schoenbrun and correspondents like Eric Sevareid would be there, and it was a very warm and relaxed occasion."

From 1954 until his retirement in 1961, news director Sig Michelson was the CIA-designated contact at CBS. With Michelson's retirement, his successor, Richard Salant, took up many of the same responsibilities. Salant even served on a secret Agency task force on China in 1964 and 1965. Salant also presided over the "CBS News Inquiry: The Warren Report" series broadcast in June, 1967. Salant had received the go-ahead for the Warren programs at a CBS executive board meeting in December, 1966.

There is no direct evidence to indicate that the program was discussed, however, just a few weeks later at the annual New Year's Day party the Agency regularly hosted for its special friends at CBS.

A Visit from the Bayou

The Sylvia Odio Controversy

Published by Bobbs-Merrill in 1967, Sylvia Meagher's *Accessories After The Fact* remains to this day the definitive critique of the Warren Report.

As the most important scholar ever to emerge from the critic's community, Meagher's contribution was encyclopedic in both scope and detail. Not only does she uniquely and efficiently demolish the Warren Commission's Lone Gunman theory; toward the conclusion of her book Meagher provides the basis for an alternative accounting of Kennedy's murder. For her, something essential still lurked in the contradictions already known to conspiracy theorists as the Second Oswald controversy.

The crux of the problem was this: after Oswald's arrest, more than a dozen people had notified government officials about odd contacts they'd had in the weeks prior to the assassination with a man who called himself Lee Harvey Oswald, or a variant of same. These "sightings" had all occurred when the real Lee Harvey Oswald was accounted for in other locations.

Meagher recounts that while the real Oswald was home with his wife, and landlady Ruth Paine, someone claiming to be Oswald was:

- leaving a rifle he would never reclaim at an Irving gunshop on November 7, 1963;

- cashing a $189 dollar check—an amount large enough to be memorable—in a small Irving grocery store on November 8;

- bragging to a Lincoln car dealer in Dallas on November 9 about the large amount of money he was about to receive (Oswald didn't drive);

- showing up regularly, beginning on November 10, at the Sports Drome Rifle Range in Dallas.

• sending a telegram to Washington D.C., possibly to the Department of the Navy, causing Western Union night manager C.A. Hamblen to recall that this was the same guy who had been receiving small amounts of money from this same Western Union office for quite some time.

Either the real Oswald possessed an uncanny ability to be in two places at once, or somebody impersonating Oswald was going out of his way to leave a trail of incriminating evidence leading up to the assassination.

THE PATTERN MAY HAVE begun when three scruffy, travel-weary men showed up at the door of Sylvia Odio's Dallas apartment one evening in September, 1963. Odio was the daughter of one of Castro's political prisoners, and she had organized a Dallas chapter of JURE (Junta Revolucionaria), a moderate, left-leaning, anti-Castro Cuban exile political organization which her father had first organized in Miami.

The three men identified themselves as fellow JURE members. Convinced by their background knowledge of past JURE activities, Odio invited them into her apartment. The spokesman of the group, "Leopoldo," and another man, "Angelo"—were either Mexicans or Cubans, Odio thought. The third man was an American. He was introduced to Odio as "Leon."

Talking to Odio by telephone the next day, "Leopoldo" explained that "Leon" was an ex-Marine; a crack rifle shot; someone who strongly believed that John Kennedy should be killed for his betrayal of the Cuban cause at the Bay of Pigs; and a man who would do anything for the chance to kill Castro.

Two months later, on the night of the Kennedy assassination, when a picture of the President's alleged assassin was flashed on the television screen, Odio and her sister Annie Laurie Odio—who had also been present during

Meagher, Sylvia

I n Sylvia Meagher, a research analyst for the World Health Organization, the assassination found a critic who had mastered the detail of both the Warren Report and the 26 volumes of supporting testimony to a degree unparalleled by most Warren staffers, let alone any of the distinguished Warren Commissioners.

Meagher's fascination with the Report, and her concern for its most minuscule detail, initially led her to create an index for all Commission documents, something the goverment had not deemed necessary for readers. As professor Peter Dale Scott, a former Canadian diplomat, has said: "If [Meagher] had written nothing else, she would have been remembered for the way this index drew order out of chaos, defined a subject matter for serious scholarship and invited anyone who cared to drive a wedge between the findings of the Warren Report, and [the actual evidence to be found in] its own twenty-six volumes of published Hearings."

In compiling *Accessories After the Fact*, Meagher's thematic approach was everywhere: the Commission had chosen to overlook the contradictions inherent in the evidence. In reaching its conclusions, the Commissioners had chosen to dwell exclusively on testimony and evidence which best reinforced a single assassin scenario.

Meagher wasn't the first critic to reach this conclusion. She was simply the first critic to reach this conclusion with a full command of all the evidence.

the men's visit—nearly went through the floor when they recognized Lee Harvey Oswald. It was "Leon."

Upon learning of Ms. Odio's experience, the FBI swarmed the story. The Commission's official Oswald chronology would place him as just arriving, or still en route, to Mexico at the time of "Leon's" visit to Odio. But Odio's background held up, and Warren staffers were hard pressed to find any way, or reason, to dismiss her story.

Only when J. Edgar Hoover claimed to have found the three men who had visited Odio—and announced that none of these men were in fact Oswald—did the Warren Commission lose interest in Ms. Odio's account. The FBI later learned that it had been wrong; the three men they had found in California were not the men who had visited Odio, but it was too late to do much about it, as the Commission's report was already on its way to the printer.

Once again the Commission had been asked to choose between two ominous choices. One of these men could have been Oswald—in which case the Commission had just discovered the roots of a real conspiracy. Or a Second Oswald was in the business of setting up the real Oswald to take the fall for the forthcoming assassination, revealing an even more complex conspiracy. Resorting to form, the Commission let the point dangle, and never again returned to it.

The final sighting of the Second Oswald took place on the day of the assassination. He may have been the man at least three witnesses had seen run down the back slope of the Book Depository after the shooting and jump into a Nash Rambler driven by a dark-skinned [Cuban?] man. This second man couldn't have been Oswald. At that time, according to the Commission's account, the real Lee Harvey Oswald had already embarked on his well chronicled, Odysseus-like journey to the awaiting Ithaca of the Texas Theater.

SYLVIA MEAGHER THUS BELIEVED THAT THE TRAIL to Kennedy's killers might be uncovered by a far more rigorous examination of the strange adventures of this other phantom Oswald. For Meagher, Sylvia Odio's testimony—particularly her background in the anti-Castro Cuban underground—seemed a particularly inviting place to start.

The "Only A Hobo" Conspiracy Theory

Moments after the assassination, the FBI detained four suspects whose presence in Dealey Plaza has haunted many conspiracy buffs ever since. One suspect was Eugene Brading, a California con-man with active associations among the Dallas Mob, and a reputed courier for Carlos Marcello. Three exceptionally well-dressed "tramps" were also picked up in the railroad yards behind the plaza. Critics have had a field day attempting to identify these men. Some candidates have included Maj. Gen. Edward Lansdale, former Saigon station chief for the CIA and an architect of the Bay of Pigs invasion; the mysterious "Raoul," said by James Earl Ray to have masterminded the death of Martin Luther King; E. Howard Hunt and Frank Sturgis, who have gone to court to successfully clear their names of this charge; and a wide assortment of Dallas mobsters, and French and American intelligence operatives. One small-time Dallas hood, Charles Harrelson, father of Cheers actor Woody Harrelson, has even confessed to the murder of JFK.

The Road Back to New Orleans

The Anti-Castro Cubans Controversy

 **A**nswers to the perplexing Two Oswald phenomena, Sylvia Meagher suggested, might be found in the underground of Cuban political exiles still attempting, with the CIA's help, to overthrow Castro's government in Havana.

"In the vein of pure speculation," Meagher writes in *Accessories After the Fact*, "it is possible to postulate a series of threads connecting persons known and unknown which would satisfy the conditions for [a] successful [Oswald] impersonation. The starting point is the summer of 1963, when Oswald came into contact with Carlos Bringuier and others who were active in the organized anti-Castro movement.

Bringuier, ostensibly a New Orleans shopkeeper, was a leading figure in the anti-Castro Cuban exile community. "Oswald sought out Bringuier under circumstances which suggest a calculated attempt to infiltrate the anti-Castro movement, perhaps in the hope of acquiring "credentials" for a future defection to Cuba. That is how Bringuier regarded the incident," Meagher writes.

"Bringuier alerted other anti-Castroites against Oswald. One of Bringuier's cohorts went on an infiltration mission of his own, after consulting Bringuier. He went to Oswald's house "posing as a pro-Castro" to "try to get as much information as possible from Oswald. It is thus a reasonable assumption that a warning against Oswald went out to the right- wing of the anti-Castro movement in other cities, and to their American sponsors and supporters, both official (CIA and perhaps FBI) and unofficial (various ultra-reactionary groups).

"The right-wing Cuban emigres were bitter and infuriated by the humiliating defeat at the Bay of Pigs, blaming President Kennedy for refusing to permit direct American military participation in the invasion. The CIA, whose conduct of the whole affair brought the agency into disgrace and jeopardy, had made arrangements to overrule President Kennedy if he canceled the invasion at the last minute, so that the landing at the Bay of Pigs would go ahead regardless of Presidential orders. The revelation that the CIA had contemplated countermanding the White House, on top of its incredible bungling of the invasion from beginning to end, suggested an early end to what has been called 'the invisible government,' and a threat to their Cuban proteges.

"Dallas, with its hospitable political climate and its plentiful money, inevitably was an outpost of the anti-Castro right wing. Sylvia Odio testified that the Crestwood Apartments, where she lived at the time of the visit by "Leon Oswald" was "full of Cubans." Fund-raising meetings were held in a Dallas bank by

Cuban exiles and their American sympathizers.

"Father Walter J. McChann, who was active in a Cuban Catholic committee concerned with the welfare and relief of Cuban refugees in Dallas, told the Secret Service about a Colonel Caster who was associated with the committee. Father McChann said that Colonel Caster was a retired Army officer who seemed to be "playing the role of an intelligence officer in his contacts with the Cubans" and that he seemed to be "more interested in their political beliefs than in their economic plight or their social problems in the new country."

Mrs. C. L. Connell, a volunteer worker in the committee, also mentioned the Colonel. She told the FBI on November 29, 1963 that during the preceding months "General Walker and Colonel Caster, a close acquaintance of Walker, have been trying to arouse the feelings of the Cuban refugees in Dallas against the Kennedy administration" in speeches before Cuban exile groups in Dallas.

MEAGHER was intrigued by this web of associations. "At this point," she writes, "a hyphothetical series of links connects Oswald to Bringuier—Bringuier to the anti-Castro movement in Dallas—the anti-Castro movement to Colonel Caster—and Colonel Caster to General Walker. Walker's right hand-man is Robert Allan Surrey. According to Surrey's own statement, he and FBI Agent James Hosty [who was monitoring Oswald's behavior in the weeks before the assassination] are bridge-playing companions."

Other trails led from General Walker to Jack Ruby, Meagher contends. "A former employee of the General's, William McEwan Duff, believed that he had seen Ruby visiting the Walker residence. There is strong evidence that Ruby was involved in the illegal supply of arms to the Cuban underground. Ruby, of course, had close links to the Dallas police, some of whom had independent links to the ultra-right in Dallas. J.D. Tippit, for example, had a moonlighting job at Austin's Barbecue; the man who was his boss, Austin Cook, is an acknowledged member of the Dallas John Birch Society.

"All these threads can be combined in a web that covers the terrible and unfathomed events of November 22-24, 1963," Meagher speculates. "The nucleus consists of reactionary Cuban exiles who have compiled a record of violence in their new country, ranging from attacks with bicycle chains and Molotov cocktails on peacefully assembled American citizens, to a bazooka attack on the United Nations building; these Cuban counterrevolutionaries are linked to the American ultra-right by many mutual interests, not the least of which was a hatred for President Kennedy, kept at the boiling point by systematic propaganda from, among others, former Army officers."

"Is it farfetched," Meagher asks in conclusion, "to postulate the formation of a plot among members of those circles to revenge themselves not only against the President whom they considered a Communist and a traitor, but also against a Marxist and suspected double-agent who had tried to infiltrate the anti-Castro movement?"

That question would lurk for decades at the core of the assassination debate.

The Dallas Cuban Connection

By the time of John Kennedy's November, 1963 visit to Dallas, the political landscape of the Caribbean coastal region—from Miami west to Dallas—had largely been reshaped by a series of political seismic shocks which began almost four years earlier, on New Year's Day, 1959. That was the day communist revolutionary Fidel Castro came down from the mountains and seized power in Cuba. Castro's ascent set in motion a wave of emigration, as hundreds of thousands of Cubans, particularly those affiliated with the ousted Batista government, set sail for a new home in the United States.

Along with tens of thousands of normal working class people, America would also absorb the remnants of a police state government which American dollars—particularly American gangster and drug dollars—had helped install in Cuba in the first place. Along with returning casino operators and narcotics dealers, southern cities such as Miami, New Orleans, and Dallas would now make way for a veritable invasion of Cuban paramilitary men and police officers who had once enforced the policies of Batista's tidy little police state. The chickens, as they say, had come to roost.

New anti-Castro Cuban paramilitary cells, comprised mainly of former cops, national guardsmen and casino security forces, were quickly assembled in the streets of America's southern cities. Trained by the CIA, these groups would provide the foot soldiers when JFK reluctantly gave the go-ahead for the April, 1961 invasion at Cuba's Bay of Pigs. Kennedy had been in power only three months when he found himself pressured into this counter-revolutionary paramilitary operation. Unnerved by the prospect of letting the CIA run roughshod over his authority,

Carlos Bringuier

Kennedy declined to provide air cover for the anti-Castro forces, and the invasion quickly turned into a disaster on Cuban shores, as the outnumbered CIA forces were easily routed.

Kennedy's ambivalent behavior was still being hotly debated when the Cuban Missile Crisis erupted in the fall of 1962. After the failure at the Bay of Pigs, Kennedy had launched his own secret anti-Castro paramilitary plan—Operation Mongoose. It was, if anything, even more sinister than what the CIA had previously attempted. But before Operation Mongoose could reach fruition, the entire hemisphere was plunged into the deadly standoff of the October missile crisis. In order to protect Castro's communist regime, the Soviet Union sent ships to Cuba loaded with warheads that could easily reach U.S. soil. Kennedy resolved the crisis by promising Castro, and the Soviet Union, that the U.S. would curtail support of the exiles' attempts to recapture their homeland.

The Cuban exile community turned on Kennedy with a vengeance. By spring, 1963, Kennedy had inherited a classic political dispersal problem: what do you do with the revolutionaries—counter-revolutionaries, in this instance—once the revolution is finished? By the summer of 1963, with the financial assistance of some former Havana casino mob bosses, several Cuban paramilitary groups decided to continue the battle, whether John Kennedy liked it or not. For the most violent members of these groups, it would be easy enough to train their guns at JFK, if he decided to interfere.

Miami would remain the capital city of the anti-Castro obsession. But by the summer of 1963, strong outposts had sprung up in both New Orleans and Dallas. The paramilitary organization which Sylvia Odio's father had helped found, and to which Odio herself belonged—Junta Revolucionaria (JURE)—was quite active in Dallas. So was Carlos Bringuier's growing organization, the Revolutionary Student Directorate (DRE). While JURE was so far to the left it was considered "Communism Without Castro," both JURE and DRE were violence-prone.

The MOST VIOLENT OF all the exile groups, however, was Alpha 66. At the time Sylvia Odio received a man she would later identify as Lee Harvey Oswald into her home, Odio's father was in a Cuban jail, accused of harboring from Castro one of Alpha 66's two founders, Reinaldo Gonzales. As it turned out, Alpha 66 was operational in Dallas at the time of the Kennedy assassination. Its chapter leader was a man named Manuel Rodriquez.

In appearance, Rodriguez was con-sidered a dead-ringer for Oswald. Some assassination theorists believe that Rodriguez must have been the man mistaken for Oswald at the DRE meeting that summer at which General Walker was first asked to speak. The plot thickened when it was later learned that the gun shop where Rodriguez regularly purchased ammunition for Alpha 66 training exercises was one of only two shops in Dallas where it was possible to buy ammunition for the rare Mannlicher-Carcano rifle.

The other founder of Alpha 66 was a man by the name of Antonio Veciana, who was a regular visitor to Dallas during 1963. Veciana would later attest that during one of his trips to Dallas he had seen Lee Harvey Oswald in the company of his own CIA handler, a man by the name of Maurice Bishop. Details of the Bishop-Oswald relationship would not emerge, however, until 1979, when Gaeton Fonzi brought the information to the House Select Committee on Assassinations investigation into JFK's murder.

For the purposes of our story, it is important to note here only that Sylvia Meagher had intuited something very significant in her attention to the Dallas/New Orleans Cuban connection.

The Road Back to New Orleans

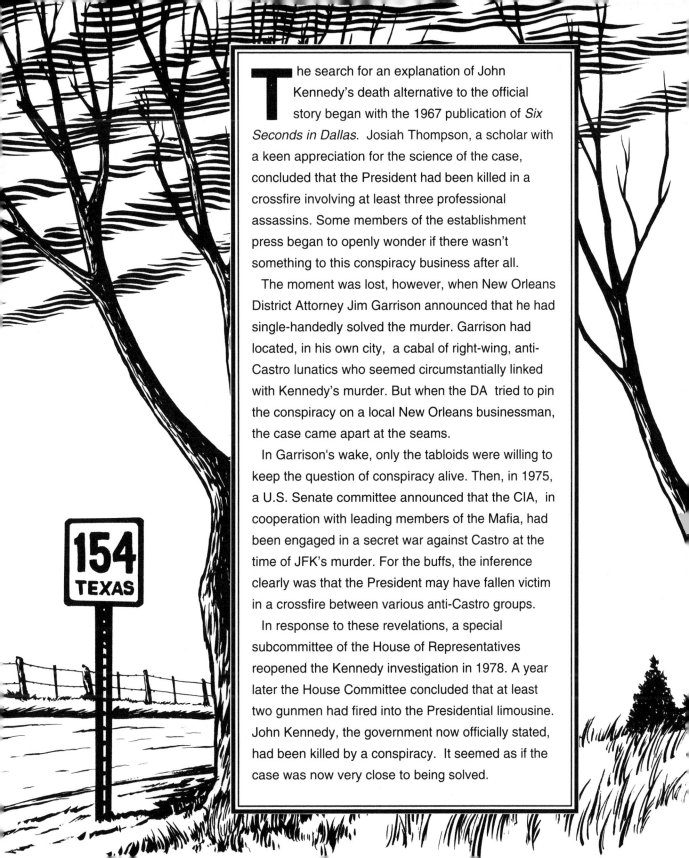

The search for an explanation of John Kennedy's death alternative to the official story began with the 1967 publication of *Six Seconds in Dallas*. Josiah Thompson, a scholar with a keen appreciation for the science of the case, concluded that the President had been killed in a crossfire involving at least three professional assassins. Some members of the establishment press began to openly wonder if there wasn't something to this conspiracy business after all.

The moment was lost, however, when New Orleans District Attorney Jim Garrison announced that he had single-handedly solved the murder. Garrison had located, in his own city, a cabal of right-wing, anti-Castro lunatics who seemed circumstantially linked with Kennedy's murder. But when the DA tried to pin the conspiracy on a local New Orleans businessman, the case came apart at the seams.

In Garrison's wake, only the tabloids were willing to keep the question of conspiracy alive. Then, in 1975, a U.S. Senate committee announced that the CIA, in cooperation with leading members of the Mafia, had been engaged in a secret war against Castro at the time of JFK's murder. For the buffs, the inference clearly was that the President may have fallen victim in a crossfire between various anti-Castro groups.

In response to these revelations, a special subcommittee of the House of Representatives reopened the Kennedy investigation in 1978. A year later the House Committee concluded that at least two gunmen had fired into the Presidential limousine. John Kennedy, the government now officially stated, had been killed by a conspiracy. It seemed as if the case was now very close to being solved.

Thompson next considered the possibility that Jacqueline Kennedy had grabbed the President in her arms after impact, accounting for the sudden backward snap of his head. But no, Thompson noted—Mrs. Kennedy was clearly unable to pull the President's body out of the line of fire this early in the film.

Thompson then considered the possibility that the Presidential limousine had suddenly accelerated or decelerated at this time. The film showed that yes, the limousine had indeed slowed down, then had speeded up—but only after the impact of this mysterious head shot.

P ERHAPS MEDICAL SCIENCE COULD PROVIDE AN answer. Could the headsnap be some sort of neuromuscular reaction? Unlikely, the author learned. "Even if this area of the head did excite some nerve impulse before it was torn from the brain," Thompson came to realize after discussing the matter with a respected neurologist, "the resultant movement would be general and random; it would not throw the President's body in any particular direction... the expected neurological effect of such a shot in the head would in fact be for the victim's entire body to go limp."

Thompson was running out of explanations for the mysterious movement of the President's head. Perhaps there was some physical principle or law of nature that could explain it. Again Thompson reached a dead end. The principle of physics that would prevail in such circumstances, he learned, would have to be Newton's second law of motion, which states that the rate of change of momentum is proportional to the impressed force, and is in the direction in which the force acts. According to UCLA physics professor A.J. Riddle, this meant that if someone is shot, and the shot strikes bone, the general direction of recoil would be away from—not toward—the shooter.

Thompson was down to his last explanation. It was simple, but its implications were truly frightening: somewhere between Zapruder frames 312 and 314, the President had been shot again. One shot had been fired from the rear (causing the initial forward movement); the second shot had been fired from in front of the President, somewhere to his right.

Standing in Dealey Plaza at the exact site of the shooting, Thompson looked back up Elm Street, to the Texas School Book Depository. He then looked down Elm, to the right— at a wooden fence atop the grassy knoll.

The "Curse of the Mole Men" Conspiracy Theory

As was often the case in the early days of conspiracy research, sophisticated investigative work such as Josiah Thompson's was soon balanced in the public's mind with the more imaginative promptings of critics like Lillian Castellano, who suggested that one of the President's assassins may have popped out of a storm drain on Elm Street. Critic David Lifton took Castellano's suspicion once step further, suggesting that prior to the assassination the grassy knoll had been excavated and tunnels and bunkers had been built underneath to allow the assassins to move about at will. Lifton even went so far as to speculate that the famous "puff of smoke" may have been exhaust from a gas engine built into the base of the knoll.

Caught in the Crossfire

The Three Assassins Controversy

A combination of hard fact and educated speculation, *Six Seconds in Dallas* concludes with the following reconstruction of the assassination of President Kennedy. It would have been relatively easy for three assassins to have reached their firing locations by 12:30, Josiah Thompson contended. By 12:30, the first assassin was in position at the sixth-floor window of the Depository. The second assassin was in position on the roof of an adjacent building. And the third assassin had taken up his position behind the stockade fence in the rear of the grassy knoll.

As for the assassin inside the Texas School Book Depository, Thompson accepts the testimony of eyewitnesses Arnold Rowland, Ronald Fischer and Bob Edwards. Each had looked up to the sixth floor of the building in the moments before the assassination, and each saw a man standing in the window overlooking Dealey Plaza. According to Rowland, the man was wearing "a very light-col-ored shirt ... open at the collar." He was also cradling a rifle.

But was it Lee Harvey Oswald? A depository secretary, Mrs. R. E. Arnold, claimed to have seen a man who looked like Oswald on the first floor of the building at 12:15. Twenty minutes later, Oswald would be discovered on the second floor, eating in the lunchroom. For Thompson, it was an open question whether the man on the sixth floor with the rifle was Oswald. Whoever it was, he was about to use Oswald's gun.

Shortly after 12:30 the sixth floor shooter looked out the window to see the President's limousine turn from Main onto Houston, and begin its slow crawl down Houston toward its next turn, directly in front of the Depository. Looking toward the motorcade as it approached, the rifleman could clearly see Kennedy smiling at Mrs. Connally. If this assassin was operating alone, now was certainly the best time to open fire.

"The gunman on the sixth floor had, however, sighted in on the agreed-upon spot just opposite the Stemmons Freeway sign," Thompson maintained. "Hidden for a moment in the foliage of an oak tree, the limousine slowly emerged at a speed of eleven miles an hour. The gunman saw the President's back and shoulders appear in his scope and carefully aligned the cross hairs. Rifle stock pressed close to his cheek, the barrel braced against a cardboard box, he squeezed the trigger."

The first shot hit the President in the shoulder. Slightly more than a half second later, Governor Connally turned to see what had happened. The President could now be seen reacting to his back wound. Slightly more than a full second after the President had been first hit, a second shot rang out, and Governor Connally collapsed into his wife's arms, seriously wounded.

Six eyewitnesses would later tell the Warren Commission that one of the bullets had been fired from the general direction of the Dal-Tex building. Based on his examination of the physical evidence, Thompson concluded that the eyewitnesses had been right: the second bullet had been fired by a separate assassin located atop either the Dal-Tex or Criminal Courts building.

At this point, however, the President had not yet been fatally wounded. The sixth floor assassin aimed and fired again. The President's body jerked

1-Location of limousine when Kennedy is first struck in the back.
2-Location of limousine when Kennedy is hit by fatal head shot. Connally is wounded somewhere between these two spots.
A- "Oswald" window of School Book Depository

B- The Dal-Tex Building. Weisberg believed a sniper was located here.
C- The Criminal Courts Building- Thompson thought that the Connally bullet may have come from here or the Dal-Tex Building.
D- The stockade fence: possible source of the final, fatal head shot.

forward for a micro-second, and then backwards—as the third assassin fired what may have been a high-powered long-barreled pistol from behind the stockade fence, some forty yards away. The President's brain was blown out of his head. Mrs. Kennedy and the two motorcycle escorts riding to the left rear of the limousine were covered in the resulting debris.

Now all three assassins had to make their escape. The rooftop assassin, Thompson speculates, simply faded into the crowd, as attention had been drawn to either the Book Depository or grassy knoll.

As for the shooter behind the fence, Thompson wondered if one of the two men Lee Bowers saw standing at the fence hadn't, immediately after the shooting, opened the trunk of his car so the shooter could climb inside, hidden from the crowd that soon congregated. The driver of the car, Thompson suggests, may very well have been the mysterious Secret Service agent whom Officer J.M. Smith briefly talked with upon arriving at the site. In the confusion, the two men simply drove away.

As the Grassy Knoll assassins left the railroad yard, and as the Dal-Tex shooter lost himself in the crowd, eyewitness Richard Carr saw the man he had previously seen on the sixth floor of the depository come out of the building, and get into a light-colored Rambler station wagon. The driver, Carr testified, was a "Negro." Carr was not alone in his observation. Deputy Sheriff Roger Craig and motorist Richard Robinson also saw a man run down the grassy incline in front of the depository, and climb into a Rambler station wagon.

Craig later claimed that the man he saw looked like Oswald. As it is possible to account for the real Oswald's whereabouts at this time, this Oswald look-alike may or may not have been the "double" who had been moving about Dallas in the weeks leading up to the assassination. Craig also identified the Rambler driver as a "Negro," or "a dark-complected white man." The Rambler swung down Houston, took the turn at Elm, and proceeeded to disappear through the triple underpass before anyone was able to stop the car to find out if "Negro" or "a dark complected white man" didn't, in this instance, mean the same thing as Cuban.

On the Ramparts

Warren Hinckle's *Ramparts* magazine had by 1967 replaced M.S. Aroni's *A Minority of One* as the journal of record for the Kennedy Assassination debate. Under Hinckle's stewardship the magazine lived up to its title, charging wildly into the gamut of heresies now infusing the JFK murder case. New Orleans District Attorney Jim Garrison first found a sympathetic national audience through the pages of *Ramparts*. So did a cantankerous Midlothian, Texas country newspaper editor named Penn Jones, who would become noted for his dossiers on "disappearing" witnesses in the JFK and Tippit murder cases.

An extraordinary newsstand success, *Ramparts* weaved Kennedy assassination articles into a muckraking tapestry which included defiant opposition to the growing war in Vietnam and defiant support for the civil rights movement which, at the time, was encountering violent resistance in the major capitals of the American south. *Ramparts* soon became the most important political magazine of the combustible 1960s era.

In its January 1967 edition, Hinckle published a special report devoted to *Ramparts'* ten-month investigation of JFK's murder. The piece was researched and written by UCLA graduate student David Lifton, then edited into shape by David Welsh. Hinckle initially rejected the report "because it read like a goddamn legal brief." Legal brief or not, Lifton and Welsh's *The Case for Three Assassins* covered in twenty-two pages much of the same ground Josiah Thompson would later cover more expansively in *Six Seconds In Dallas. Ramparts* now also concluded that three assassins—not counting accomplices—had conspired in the murder of John Kennedy.

The Camp Street Cabal

The David Ferrie/Guy Banister Controversy

While *Accessories After The Fact* and *Six Seconds in Dallas* would remain two of the best books ever written about the assassination of JFK, the significance of their publication was overshadowed by news from New Orleans. On March 1, 1967, New Orleans District Attorney Jim Garrison announced that the JFK murder case had been cracked; he indicted Clay Shaw, a prominent local businessman, as the architect of the crime.

In *Six Seconds in Dallas*, Josiah Thompson suggested the case belonged to anyone who could identify the men behind the fence in Dallas, Texas. Garrison wasn't sure who the men behind the fence were. But he was convinced that two days after the assassination he had interrogated the back-up pilot for the assassins' escape.

The pilot's name was David Ferrie, and he was a very strange man. The son of an Irish Catholic police captain, Ferrie had been born in Cleveland in 1918. Devoutly religious throughout his life, Ferrie had entered a Catholic seminary as a teenager. He didn't last long in the seminary, however, as Ferrie was also an ardent homosexual. Church fathers asked him to leave, due to what they euphemistically called the problem of his "emotional instability."

Ferrie's intellectual life, however, burned brightly.

In 1941 he received a bachelor's degree in philosophy from Baldwin-Wallace College. After college, he devoted his life to becoming a successful airline pilot. When he was hired by Eastern Airlines, Ferrie moved to New Orleans, where in addition to his new pilot duties, he became the leader of the local chapter of the Civil Air Patrol. In 1955, he welcomed into his Air Patrol chapter a fatherless, New Orleans teenager, who lived with his mother above a pool hall at 126 Exchange Place, in the middle of one of the town's most crime-ridden neighborhoods. The young man's name was Lee Harvey Oswald.

BY THE MID-50S FERRIE'S PENCHANT FOR PHIlosophy had become increasingly political. By the end of the decade, he would be known throughout New Orleans as one of the city's most strident anti-Communists. In a town of unique characters, Ferrie would become renowned as one of the most "colorful." During the late 1950s, Ferrie's path first crossed with two other rabid anti-Communists, W. Guy Banister, a former FBI agent from Chicago, and Sergio Arcacha Smith, a former diplomat in the Batista administration in Cuba. They too were extraordinary characters.

In New Orleans, Arcacha had become local representative for the Cuban Revolutionary Council (CRC), an umbrella organization comprised of militant anti-Castro exiles first assembled in Miami by CIA agent E. Howard Hunt in anticipation of the Bay of Pigs invasion. Both Banister and Arcacha had been active in that ill-fated operation. Both men continued in the movement thereafter by helping to train militant Cuban exiles, and various neo-Nazi soldiers of fortune, at a secluded ranch owned by the family of a former Havana casino operator with links to gangster Meyer Lansky. The base was located near Arcacha's home, some 30 miles from New Orleans on the northern shore of Lake Pontchartrain.

By 1961, David Ferrie's usefulness to the anti-Castro movement was temporarily inhibited by a series of arrests for sexual encounters with young boys. On August 26, 1961, the scandal had grown to the point where Eastern Airlines was compelled to put Ferrie on suspension. At that point Banister, Arcacha, and G. Wray Gill, lawyer to New Orleans mafia boss Carlos Marcello, all weighed in on Ferrie's side.

In a letter to Eastern, Arcacha offered the following appreciation of his friend Ferrie: "When the FRD (Democratic Revolutionary Front) was originally organized, under the demands of the U.S. government, the FRD was to 'front' for the effort of the CIA to reinstate democratic government in Cuba. The effort of April 17 [the Bay of Pigs] failed, as you know, thereafter the morale of the Cubans in exile, and the Underground in Cuba, fell to zero. Then along came Captain Ferrie. He strongly prodded our organization until it was revitalized. Thereafter dissident elements were removed, fund collecting began, the Underground was reorganized, and the reharassment of Castro has begun."

Carlos Marcello stepped forward to fund the exile movement at this time.

Eastern Airlines was unimpressed. Ferrie was fired for good. From that point forward, Ferrie could regularly be seen hustling in and out of both Guy Banister's offices, and those of the CRC, both of which were located on the second floor of 544 Camp Street in New Orleans.

For students of the Kennedy assassination, the second floor offices of 544 Camp Street would become enormously important. Considered a "veritable Disneyland of anti-Castro activities" by critic Philip Melanson, the Camp Street headquarters was a magnet for anti-Castro paramilitary fighters.

Captain Ferrie's former Air Cadet, Lee Harvey Oswald, had found his own way to Camp Street by the summer of 1963. Back from his own mysterious two-year sojourn inside the Soviet Union, Oswald had returned to New Orleans the previous April. On May 9, 1963 this 24 year-old Marxist ex-Marine took a job at the William B. Reily Coffee Plant just two blocks away from 544 Camp. William Reily was also an active anti-Communist, who had helped to fund various anti-Castro activities. The neighborhood was full of intrigue. Both the Secret Service and the FBI regularly parked their cars in the garage immediately across the street from Reily's coffee company.

By June, Oswald was out on the streets of New Orleans, in the heart of the virulently anti-Castro community, passing out pamphlets for the Fair Play for Cuba Committee, in support of the Castro government. The group had no known members other than Oswald.

87

Was Oswald really a supporter of Fidel Castro? Or, with his days in the Soviet Union now behind him, had he become as avidly anti-Castro as his old Cadet captain, David Ferrie? The weight of the evidence suggests that Oswald was probably on a fishing expedition, attempting to draw out and identify actual Castro supporters in the city. He was aided in this effort by what seems to have been a staged street scuffle, and a subsequent radio debate, with Carlos Bringuier, the New Orleans delegate for the anti-Castro Student Directorate (DRE). Bringuier had previously served as Sergio Arcacha's CRC press secretary—working out of 544 Camp Street. The key evidence, however, was the address which Oswald had printed on his pro-Castro pamphlets: 544 Camp Street. Either Oswald was an active accomplice of Ferrie, Banister, and Carlos Bringuier, or—not for the first time—Oswald was being used as something of a CIA-related spook, sent in to monitor the actions of this potentially rogue faction of the Castro counter-revolutionary forces.

THIS WAS THE SCENARIO JIM GARRISON began to formulate, in considerable detail, in preparation for the trial of Clay Shaw , which was scheduled to begin in January, 1969. Shaw, Garrison had become convinced, was the covert captain of the Ferrie-Banister-Arcacha-Bringuier-Oswald brigade, an active CIA conduit who had ultimately launched these forces against President Kennedy.

In hindsight, it now seems that Garrison had come extremely close to a resolution of the Kennedy assassination, only to see the core of his tenuous court case be completely blown away in the months to come.

TWO VERY DANGEROUS MEN

Harold Weisberg's *Oswald in New Orleans*, published in 1967 by Canyon Books, gathered together all of the evidence the Warren Commission had assembled—but eventually ignored—concerning Oswald's lost summer in New Orleans. Weisberg's book would be used as an initial agenda for the Garrison investigation. Then in January, 1968, *Ramparts* published former FBI agent William Turner's background story of the Garrison investigation in a book-length piece entitled *The Garrison Commission*. From Weisberg and Turner, the public first learned of the immense weirdness of David Ferrie, and of the political extremism of his associate, Guy Banister.

After being fired by Eastern, Ferrie contracted a rare skin disease called alopecia, which caused him to lose all the hair on his body. He tried to compensate by creating an ill-fitting mohair wig, and pasting on two shards of a red mohair rug for eyebrows. So adorned, Ferrie rose to second in command of the violent cadre of right wing, anti-Castro paramilitary men then gathering in and around New Orleans.

Although nowhere near as exotic a bird, Guy Banister was every bit as sinister as his colleague. Working for the FBI in Chicago, Banister had participated in the legendary shootout which killed America's "Public Enemy Number One," John Dillinger. Like Dallas D.A. Henry Wade, Banister had also worked with the Office of Naval Intelligence during World War II. It was rumored that Banister maintained contact with ONI throughout the ensuing years.

Guy Banister moved to New Orleans in 1955 to become Deputy Chief of Police. A penchant for violence, and a dependency on alcohol, ultimately ruined Banister's professional career, much as a penchant for young boys ruined David Ferrie. Fired from the New Orleans Police Department in 1957 for pistol-whipping a local waiter, Banister founded his own private detective agency and devoted himself to a variety of anti-Communist and racist causes. In short order, Banister joined the John Birch Society. He became an active member of the ultra-right Minutemen paramilitary underground network. He also published the racist *Louisiana Intelligence Digest*.

In the late 50s, Banister became the New Orleans chapter head of the Anti-Communism League of the Caribbean, another CIA front which had initially been created to overthrow the left-leaning Arbenz government in Guatemala. One of Banister's ACLC associates alleged that the League opened a pipeline with the OAS, a French criminal-influenced anti-Communist group. The ACLC, it is alleged, fed $200,000 to the OAS to help pay for the attempted assassination of French Prime Minister Charles DeGaulle.

Banister cooperated with Sergio Arcacha Smith in the training of exiles for the Bay of Pigs. Visitors to his offices, and those of the CRC across the hall, often commented on numerous boxes of small arms and explosives stored under Banister's care at 544 Camp Street.

It was Jack Martin, one of Banister's associates, who called Jim Garrison two days after the JFK assassination to inform the District Attorney of the strange activities of Guy Banister, and his fellow radical extremist, David Ferrie. It was Martin's contention, as it would become Garrison's, that Lee Harvey Oswald had been under the influence of these two very dangerous men.

The Trial of Clay Shaw

The Jim Garrison Controversy

ew Orleans District Attorney Earling Carothers "Jim" Garrison arrested Clay Shaw on March 1, 1967, for his alleged participation in a conspiracy to murder John F. Kennedy. Twenty-two months would pass before the Shaw trial would finally get underway. Twenty-two months in which the DA, and those who supported his case, filled the airwaves and bookstores with Jim Garrison's official version of the crime. Twenty-two months in which Garrison's critics—and they became legion—would combat the Gospel according to Garrison with media interviews, network "white papers," and a slew of publications contesting not only Garrison's case, but his character. In those twenty-two months, Garrison's case against Clay Shaw would steadily unravel.

Friends of Jim Garrison—and the six-foot-six "Jolly Green Giant" himself—would be the first to take their case before the court of public opinion. Following the 1967 publication of Harold Weisberg's *Oswald in New Orleans*, Garrison himself headed out on the old publicity trail. In October, Big Jim subjected himself to the longest interview in the history of *Playboy* magazine. Entitled "A Candid Conversation with the Embattled District Attorney of New Orleans," the *Playboy* interview was little more than bunny fluff for the articulate Mr. Garrison. As the title indicated, it was Garrison who came off as the victim of his own investigative process, not Clay Shaw. Egged on by comedian Mort Sahl, Garrison had also emerged triumphant from a totally surreal late night interview with Tonight Show host Johnny Carson.

THE PUBLIC CASE AGAINST GARRISON BEGAN slightly more than two weeks before the Shaw arrest, when *New Orleans States-Item* reporter Rosemary James first broke the story in the February 17, 1967 edition of her newspaper. In spite of herself, James could not help but convey the idea that it was simply incredulous that Garrison could suggest a link between the killing of the President and an old-fashioned New Orleans gentleman like Mr. Clay Shaw.

Well, James was partially right. The story was incredulous. At the time, Clay Shaw was one of the most respected members of the New Orleans civic establishment. An international businessman of note, Shaw was considered the brains behind the thriving new International Trade Mart which had helped make New Orleans the most bustling port city on the Gulf.

Shaw was also considered a one-man restoration committee in terms of the exciting architecture of the French Quarter. From 1949 until his trial in 1968, Shaw had managed to elegantly restore 16 different homes, including naturalist John James Audubon's New Orleans residence. Like his Irish namesake, Shaw was also a successful local playwright. Whether it was the theater, symphony or opera, Clay Shaw was a fixture of establishment culture in New Orleans.

Shaw had another notable interest which would provide an important subtext to his forthcoming trial. Although New Orleans was too classy a town to make much of it either way, Clay Shaw was also a marginally closeted homosexual. In fact, homosexuality, and narcotics, were never far from center stage when the focus of the Kennedy assassination shifted to New Orleans.

And so, in the early spring of 1968, these two titans of New Orleans society, DA Jim Garrison and businessman Clay Shaw, squared off against each other in what would become one of the truly sleazy events in American judicial history.

Where Big Jim had gotten off first in the publicity battle, the friends of Clay Shaw soon joined the fray in an all-out effort to counter-defame the DA. Reporter James Phelan was among the first when he wrote, in the *Saturday Evening Post* on May 15, 1967, that the DA's office had drugged and hypnotized Perry Russo, one of Garrison's key witnesses. It was Russo, on drugs, who had finally told Garrison that he had attended a party where Shaw, Ferrie and Oswald had discussed assassinating the President. The anti-Garrison attack was soon picked up by Hugh Aynesworth in *Newsweek*, and it reached critical mass with an NBC "White Paper" broadcast that June.

The battle of the press clips was a particularly important aspect of the Shaw trial. Garrison had, in fact, been compelled to bring forward his case—which was clearly not ready for trial—after Rosemary James' scoop in February. In truth, Garrison never had much of a case to begin with. Oswald was dead. Ferrie was dead, an apparent though suspicious suicide. Guy Banister had died in 1964. Sergio Arcacha Smith, living in Texas, had refused to comply with Garrison's subpoena. And, quoting Kafka, the only principal in the case still living—Clay Shaw—would deny everything.

By the time the trial began Garrison had lost most of his key witnesses either to mysterious, often violent deaths, or to a simple unwillingness to perpetuate what was quickly becoming an embarassing public charade. By the time the Judge called the proceedings to order, two of Garrison's most important staff assistants, William Gurvich and Thomas Bethell, had switched sides and were working for the Defense. One of Garrison's earliest and most vital witnesses, fat hipster lawyer Dean Andrews, now agreed to testify only on behalf of Clay Shaw's defense.

On the opening day of the trial a man showed up in court dressed solely in a toga, and informed the press that his name was "Julius Caesar." Garrison probably had a pretty good idea right then of the shape he was in.

The trial opened well enough for the prosecution. Garrison's first witnesses were a group of people from Clinton, Louisiana, who testified to having seen Oswald, Ferrie, and a man they believed was Clay Shaw visit Clinton together in the summer of 1963. The defense suggested that the man they thought was Shaw was probably Guy Banister, but the "Country People's" testimony wasn't completely discredited.

Garrison then brought to the stand Vernon Bundy, a noted local felon. Bundy testified that he had seen Oswald and Shaw during that same summer walking along the docks. "What were you doing at the time you saw these two men," the defense asked Bundy. "I was applying a torniquet on my arm in preparation for a fix," said the convicted heroin addict.

For both Garrison and Shaw, the end was coming quickly now.

A New Yorker by the name of Charles Spiesel was the next witness. Spiesel testified that while visiting his daughter, who attended a local New Orleans college, he'd had coffee with Ferrie and Shaw quite by accident, and that David Ferrie told him that he and Shaw were preparing to assassinate President Kennedy.

The defense asked Spiesel if he was in the habit of placing himself under hypnosis. Spiesel said Yes, it was true.

A murmur, as they say, was heard throughout the courtroom.

The defense stepped in a little closer. "Is it true, Mr. Spiesel, that before you sent your daughter off to college this year, you actually fingerprinted her?" "Yes, I did," Spiesel replied.

"Could you tell the jury why you fingerprinted your own daughter, Mr. Spiesel?" "Why, yes, I simply wanted to make sure it was actually her when she returned," Mr. Speisel responded.

At this exact moment, he would later recall, Garrison felt a wave of nausea rise mightily up inside, and engulf him.

The trial of Clay Shaw lasted less than five weeks. It took the jury all of 53 minutes to acquit Shaw, and kick this stinker out into the street.

HURRICANE WEATHER

THE TRIAL OF CLAY SHAW WAS A DEFINING MOMENT IN THE history of the Kennedy controversy. It relinquished the high ground in the debate back to the Lone Gunman crowd. It also split the critics like ten pins, straight down the middle. Some stood with Garrison to the end. Others believed that Garrison had always represented a major setback for the conspiracy theorist community. For the most part, the trial of Clay Shaw succeeded only in exiling the Kennedy assassination to the fourth estate's most imaginative faction: the supermarket tabloid press.

Yes, Jim Garrison was a raving egomaniac off on one of the most colossal ego trips of the modern era. The hard thing to swallow, however, was that before he became lost in one too many gay bars, Garrison was only one or two saloons away from being right on target.

The Kennedy controversy would be sustained, and its main trail would continue to run straight through New Orleans. But the man Jim Garrison had been looking for wasn't Clay Shaw. Journalist Robert Sam Anson may have been the first to publicly wonder just how different things might have turned out if the New Orleans District Attorney had turned his attention away from his glorious, over-extended vice bust, and had instead concentrated on the immense shadowy figure of New Orleans mob/narcotics boss, Carlos Marcello.

In spite of Big Jim, an ill wind could still be detected blowing through the French shutters on Camp Street.

The Gay "Thrill Kill" Theory

Reporter James Phelan would claim, under oath, that Garrison had once stated to him that John Kennedy had been a victim of a right-wing, homosexual thrill killing. "Look at the people involved," Garrison allegedly said. "David Ferrie: homosexual. Clay Shaw: homosexual. Jack Ruby: homosexual." "Ruby was a homosexual?" Phelan asked. "Sure, we dug that out," Garrison replied. "His homosexual nickname was Pinkie. That's three. Then there was Lee Harvey Oswald." But Oswald was married, with two children, Phelan protested. "A switch-hitter who couldn't satisfy his wife," Garrison declared, adding "That's all in the Warren Report." Garrison was always a big man, of course, for believing everything in the Warren Report.

25
Murder Inc. in the Caribbean

The CIA-Mafia Alliance Controversy

Johnny Roselli was sure he was about to get screwed. The U.S. government was going to deport him back to Italy. As far as Johnny was concerned, this was an act of incredibly bad faith. Hadn't he, John Roselli, in an act of incredible patriotism for his adopted country, agreed to help the CIA in one of their most sensitive programs; the secret attempt to assassinate Fidel Castro? Hadn't he, John Roselli, put together a veritable dream team of mobsters to help the CIA with this job? Not only that, hadn't he, John Roselli, along with his fellow gangsters and high-level narcotics dealers, agreed to do this job without charging the government one blessed cent?

Yes, Johnny Roselli had done all of these things. But now it was 1970, and the Immigration and Naturalization Service had Johnny's back to the wall. To avoid deportation he was forced to do what any red-blooded American criminal or politician might be expected to

do under these circumstances. He dropped his story into the awaiting arms of the always carnivorous and often gullible American press. It was of course one hell of a story—perhaps the most amazing story to emerge out of this truly lunatic political decade.

JACK ANDERSON WAS CHOSEN AS MR. ROSELli's apostle of retaliation. At the time he first met with Jack Anderson, even Johhny Roselli did not realize the larger context in which his own experiences played such a vital part. Roselli probably never knew the full story behind the Bay of Pigs. The origin of that sad saga takes us back to New Year's Day, 1959, the day that Fidel Castro seized power in Cuba.

That day thousands of officials in the Batista government—diplomats and leaders of both the police and national guard—set sail like a storm of angry hornets for new homes in and around Miami. That was the day on which American government officials in the Eisenhower administration—up to and including Richard Nixon and the CIA—first began to act a little nuts behind the threat of a new Marxist regime just 90 miles away from Florida's golden shores. And that was the day, finally, when Castro began to usurp what would eventually amount to more than $700 million worth of American-owned prop-

Nixon was placed in charge of a special National Security Task Force charged with devising a plan for an invasion of the Caribbean island. Nixon was a particularly good choice, as his own personal investments portfolio was already tied up in speculative Florida real estate deals in conjunction with various Batista officials and low-life Florida Lansky associates. In the old days, Dick Nixon had on several occasions been the guest of certain Havana gambling interests. Now, with the blessing of the White House and the help of some recently banished Mob and Cuban gambling interests, Mr. Nixon and the CIA would lead the charge to recapture this recently lost Kingdom of Pleasure, Profit and Vice.

Dirtied already by their experiences in the drug politics of Southeast Asia, a cadre of former OSS and Air America hands were given the job of organizing the new invasion force. Former OSS Colonel Paul Helliwell was chosen as paymaster for the invasion. In China , Helliwell had pioneered the art of garnering intelligence by paying off local gangsters and river pirates with opium

Greetings from HAVANA

erties in Cuba. In fact, a good deal of that property had belonged to some of Johnny Roselli's more legendary mobster friends. Meyer Lansky, Lucky Luciano, Mickey Cohen, Frank Costello, Santos Trafficante— all these men took a huge bath the day Fidel Castro took the casinos in Havana.

At the White House, President Dwight D. Eisenhower lost no time in coming up with a retaliation plan. Vice President Richard

Not since the mighty Ghengis Khan was poised at the gates of Rome had the world seen an invading force quite as mangy and strange as the one assembled by the Agency and Mr. Nixon.

sticks. In Miami, CIA official Howard Hunt was chosen to organize the exiled Cuban foot soldiers. Hunt had started his career working for Helliwell in China. Hunt's friend, William Pawley, who had put Air America's planes in the skies over China, and who had played such an important role in the Agency's skullduggery in Guatemala, was given the job of raising private off-the-shelf funds for the invading force.

On the Sicilian side of this adventure, CIA asset Frank Sturgis served as the Agency's direct link with mob boss Santos Trafficante. Sitting atop an empire built on pure heroin, Trafficante had run the mob operation in Havana under Batista. Four of Trafficante's brightest former Cuban

Casino operators—Russell Bufalino, James Plumeri, George Levine, and Salvatore Granello—would provide intelligence on Castro's troop movements right up to the invasion date. In addition to these secret gestures of a most rapacious and mutual desire, John Roselli would be asked by the CIA to help it line up a team or two of reliable hit men to simply assassinate Castro before, or during, the invasion.

Having received this request from CIA contract designate Robert Maheu at the Hilton Plaza Hotel in New York City on Sept. 14, 1960, Roselli had gone to Chicago mob boss Sam Giancana, and then to Miami-based Trafficante, seeking assistance in his "component" of the Agency's plan. The Mob was only too happy to take a whack at Castro.

Yet despite these "patriotic" efforts, the Agency was prepared to sit on its hands come 1970, and do nothing to help Johnny Roselli fight the INS's forthcoming deportation scheme. To a loyalty-bound mafioso like Roselli, this cold-shoulder treatment hardly seemed honorable. Hadn't Bobby Kennedy moved in to squash a similiar prosecution aimed at Sam Giancana back in 1962, Roselli asked. Well, yes he had. But that wasn't exactly the same thing. Sam at least had the horsesense to install one of Jack Kennedy's girlfriends, Judith Exner Campbell, into his own harem.

The Kennedy brothers couldn't move on Giancana, for the mob boss was holding at least two hot stories to feed the press if the government ever decided to put the squeeze on him. Giancana had, after all, organized a hit on a major world leader at his own government's request, and he was also sharing his bed with a woman who also shared a bed with President Kennedy. No, Johnny hadn't done nearly as good a job as Sam in protecting his own behind.

And so, in 1970, with the screws tightening on him, Roselli began to feed Jack Anderson certain details concerning his own role in the creation of a CIA-Mob army—an army which would later turn into a scandalous disaster at the Bay of Pigs. After two of these stories were released, embarrassed government officials finally got the point. The case against Johnny Roselli mysteriously evaporated. But it was too late. It's hard to put an egg back together after the shell cracks.

The Moe Howard Assassination Theory

When the CIA first sat down with Johnny Roselli, the Agency was already deploying a series of lethal devices in its efforts to kill Castro, including poisonous drugs in a wetsuit and exploding sea shells. What we'd like you guys to think about, the Agency told Johnny Roselli and Sam Giancana, is some kind of ambush involving experienced hit men armed with machine guns. "You guys have seen too many gangster movies," Giancana allegedly responded. "There is nothing at all wrong with an exploding cigar."

The New Manchurian Candidates

AT THE TIME THE CIA CONTRACTED WITH THREE MOB leaders to kill Fidel Castro, the Agency had already been in the assassination business for at least ten years. In the early days, however, the Agency had mostly concentrated on trying to create its own line of Manchurian Candidates.

The program was Project ARTICHOKE, invented for the Agency by a case officer with a taste for psychology and hypnosis by the name of Morse Allen. Starting in 1951, Allen began experimenting with his own secretaries, working the kinks out of his system. By 1954, he was ready to conduct a crucial test.

According to reporter and super sleuth John Kelly, now working with the Australian Broadcast Company, on February 19, 1954, "Allen hypnotized a CIA secretary and told her to sleep until he ordered her to awake. He then hypnotized a second secretary and instructed her that if she could not wake up her friend, "her rage would be so great that she would not hesitate to kill. Allen had left an unloaded pistol nearby, and even though the secretary had expressed a fear of weapons, she 'shot' her friend when she could not awaken her. After Allen brought her out of the trance, as programmed, the killer had amnesia and denied that she could ever kill anyone."

For the CIA, it was time to experiment in the field. The Agency had a clear idea of the kind of programmed assassin it was looking for: "an individual," as the CIA's own memos indicate, "approximately 35 years old, well-educated, proficient in English and well-established socially and politically [should best] be induced under ARTICHOKE to perform an act, involuntarily, of attempted assassination against a prominent politician or if necessary, against an American official."

The Agency left no question about what would have to be done with the shooter after the deed was done. "The Subject should be taken into custody by the govern-

ment," the memo states, "and then disposed of..."

Under the control of Allen's replacement, Sidney Gottlieb, Project ARTICHOKE turned into Project MKULTRA in the mid-1950s. The search for a Manchurian Candidate continued in the experimental science stage until 1961, when project tests were first performed in the field with a cadre of Korean Central Intelligence cadets. By the 1960s, however, the Agency had begun to think of assassination in increasingly operational terms. Sheffield Edwards, the security officer for the original ARTICHOKE project, was moved over a few desks to manage the assassination component in the ongoing plans to overthrow both Castro in Cuba, and Lumumba in the Congo. Under CIA director Richard Helms, Edwards became one of the few agents directly responsible for the six different assassination attempts—including the Roselli Project—which would be launched against Fidel Castro between the Bay of Pigs invasion until the Cuban Missile Crisis in 1962.

Rather than manufacturing Manchurian Candidates, the Agency apparently concluded, it might be more practical just to hire outside hitmen who fit the psychological profile the Agency had established.

Revolt of the Rogue Agents

The CIA Renegade Operations Controversy

After Jack Anderson's series of Johnny Roselli columns in 1971, details of the CIA-Mob Bay of Pigs alliance began to flow like an underground stream beneath the country's darkening political landscape. Lyndon Johnson replaced John Kennedy, and then Richard Nixon—the original Bay of Pigs architect—replaced Johnson. And so the river ran.

Then in 1973, E. Howard Hunt and four other Bay of Pigs veterans—Frank Sturgis, James McCord, Eugenio Martinez and Bernard Barker—were arrested burglarizing the Democratic Party suite at Washington, D.C.'s Watergate Hotel. What was Hunt looking for? everyone wondered. Hunt wouldn't talk—but The Man Who Knew Too Many Secrets announced to President Nixon that it would take a million dollars to buy his continued silence.

Nixon thought, sadly—Yes, it was a price he would have to pay.

"We protected [CIA Director Richard] Helms from one hell of a lot of things," Richard Nixon said to H.R. Haldeman in a taped White House conversation on June 23, 1972. "Of course, this Hunt, that will uncover a lot of things. You open that scab there's a hell of a lot of things... If it gets out that this is all involved, the Cuba thing, it would be a fiasco. It would make the CIA look bad, it's going to make Hunt look bad, and it is very likely to blow the whole Bay of Pigs thing, which we think would be very unfortunate—both for the CIA, and for the country... the problem is, it tracks back to the Bay of Pigs."

In truth, the "whole Bay of Pigs thing" had gotten even worse in the wake of the botched invasion. After the April, 1961 debacle, John Kennedy had not ended the secret war against Cuba. In fact, Kennedy expanded that war beyond all previous recognition. The new program would be led by the very strange General

Edward Lansdale. It would be called, in a stubborn act of poetry, Operation Mongoose, and it would become the largest CIA covert operation up to that time.

Jack Kennedy hadn't put an end to the war's assassination component either. Instead, he took it out of the hands of the Mob, and came up with a new and streamlined version, directed by CIA Case Officer William Harvey.

The new assassination component would be called ZR RIFLE. Fitting the Agency scheme, it would involve sending hired assassins into Cuba after Castro, and into the Congo after the insurgent rebel leader, Patrice Lumumba.

One of the assassins William Harvey would send into the Congo, code-named QJ/WIN, was a Corsican with a background in narcotics. QJ/WIN was never identified, but the Corsican connection was intriguing: Corsican drug lord Antoine Guerini had long been in cahoots with Cuban mob overlord Santos Trafficante. These two men had together overseen both ends of Lucky Luciano's old narcotics network. The span of their control—from Southeast Asia to the Near East, to Sicily and Marseilles to Cuba—encompassed the entire world.

Harvey also sent a second assassin—code-named AM/LASH—into Cuba after Castro. Today we know that AM/LASH was a former Castro cabinet minister by the name of Rolando Cubela, who had allegedly turned on Castro without the communist leader's knowledge, thereby retaining regular access to Castro's inner circle.

OPERATION MONGOOSE WAS GOING FULL THROTtle when Kennedy's policy toward Cuba shifted again after the Cuban Missile Crisis of April, 1962. In return for Khrushchev's removal of the controversial missiles, Kennedy pledged that the United States would abandon plans for any future invasions.

Kennedy began to make good on his promise in the early days of 1963. Operation Mongoose was terminated, and with it went the "official" Agency relationship with AM/LASH. Even as the FBI boarded up the training bases, however, it became clear that Kennedy had unleashed forces over which he had lost control.

The details of this history surfaced with the publication of the Church Committee Report in 1976. That

The Immaculate Deception Invasion Theory

Edward Lansdale, the general chosen to head up Operation Mongoose, was a remarkably inventive man. A master of dark and deceptive "psy-ops" (psychologial operations), Lansdale devised a plan in which a submarine would surface off the shores of Cuba a day or so before the actual invasion. By that time the region would have been blanketed with an announcement proclaiming the second coming of Jesus Christ, an act intended to profoundly affect the island's residents, most of whom were peasant Catholics. The submarine would contribute to their anxiety by hosting a fantastic Second Coming light show to be played out in the night sky above the island. The idea never got off the ground, however, because—in the words of the irrascible Warren Hinckle—while one bearded leader on the island of Cuba might have been okay, the idea of two bearded leaders would have been just too much.

committee had been formed to investigate covert assassination plots against leaders around the globe. Its revelations shocked the nation. For the first time, people learned that despite Kennedy's edict, and possibly without the knowledge of his CIA Director—the war against Castro had continued under the direction of a number of very angry, rogue CIA case officers.

One of these men, case officer "Maurice Bishop," served as liaison with Alpha 66, the most militant of all the CIA-funded Cuban exile groups, which spearheaded a series of new raids against the Cuban mainland. ZR/RIFLE director William Harvey also proceeded with the AM/LASH plan. Rolando Cubela was, in fact, being briefed by the CIA on November 22, 1963 at the exact moment the news of Kennedy's murder reached the Agency.

At that same moment in Harlem, Malcolm X is reported to have said, "The chickens have come home to roost."

Which Way the Mongoose Flies

According to journalist Warren Hinckle, when John Kennedy decided to visit his family's compound at West Palm Beach in the days following the Bay of Pigs fiasco, the young President was greeted by his very angry father, who said, "Son, you really blew it this time." The elder Kennedy had lost a valuable Coca-Cola franchise when Castro came down from the mountains, and now he was really steaming. In a manner long admired by the hard men of their tribe, the Brothers Kennedy suddenly got religion. 'Don't get mad, get even,' or so Hinckle alleges, became their new war cry.

Whatever the theological implications, the new anti-Castro program the Kennedy brothers created turned downtown Miami into a veritable cold-war Zurich within the year. By 1962, the Agency's car pool had more vehicles assigned to it than did the local Hertz.

The new program—this Operation Mongoose—was huge.

Composed of demothballed subchasers, converted patrol craft, hopped-up speed boats, and super-charged pleasure cruisers, the fleet the CIA assembled for Operation Mongoose became overnight the largest Navy in the Caribbean.

Working with an abandoned fleet of old World War II B-26 bombers, Cuban exile pilots were trained by experienced CIA hands from Air America, and began flying under various business fronts from commercial airports in the southeast. The bombers also flew from isolated airstrips in Florida and Louisiana, and from improvised runways hacked out of the jungles of Guatemala, Nicaragua, and Costa Rica.

"The CIA's Cuban exile soldiers," Hinckle and his co-author William Turner remark in their book *The Fish is Red*, "were equipped from the Agency's own arms supply depots in Missouri and Virginia. They received basic training in a half dozen states: Cuban pilots practiced precision supply drops at the Marana air base in Arizona; officers were schooled both at the Farm, a CIA training center located at Camp Peary near Williamsburg, Virginia, and at Fort Benning in Georgia;

Cuban frogmen were taught the art of underwater demolition at the CIA's secret Isolation Tropic base on the North Carolina coast; Cuban enlisted men were trained both at Kendell, south of Miami, and at Sergio Arcacha's CRC training base on the shores of Lake Pontchartrain.

The CIA Miami Station—which soon became the largest CIA station in the world—was code-named JM/WAVE. It was headquartered on the remote south campus of the University of Miami, inside a dummy corporation with the phony name of Zenith Technical Enterprises, Inc. The new station chief was 34 year-old Theodore Shackley. He had previously been assigned to ZR/RIFLE chief William Harvey's former CIA station in Berlin. Henry Kissinger had worked for the CIA in Berlin during that time. Now both of these cold warriors were reunited in Miami for the next stage of the war against Castro.

This time the Kennedy brothers had come to play. Their renewed efforts would provoke unexpected, and fatal, results.

The Nine Lives of Ozzie The Rabbit

The "Who Was Lee Harvey Oswald?" Controversy

Publication of the Church Committee Report proved to be a wake-up call for JFK assassination critics. What the Shaw trial had taken away with one hand, the Church Committee returned with the other. While the details of the association would be challenged, it was now clear that Lee Harvey Oswald's adventures in New Orleans had somehow been entangled in the CIA's covert assassination plots—what President Lyndon Johnson had called "that goddamn Murder Incorporated in the Caribbean." Lo and behold, Jim Garrison had been at least partially right: there had been teams of paramilitary CIA-trained gunmen murking up the streets of Miami, Dallas and New Orleans in the last days of Lee Harvey Oswald.

And so it was to Oswald, again, that the controversy returned in the months immediately following the release of the Church Committee Report. As the idea had first

been advanced by the anti-Castro paramilitaries—Howard Hunt, Frank Sturgis, and Carlos Bringueir—the Church Report seemed to support the view that Castro, working with double agents planted in the exile movement, had ordered the death of JFK in retaliation for the various attempts on his own life, and for the ongoing exile raids still being launched against Cuba from the U.S.

IN RETROSPECT, REMARKS MADE BY Fidel Castro on September 8, 1963, now seemed prophetic in both substance and tone. "We are prepared to fight them [the exile leaders], and answer in kind. United States leaders should think that if they are aiding terrorist plans to eliminate Cuban leaders... they themselves will not be safe."

The Warren Report had already ruled out any formal involvement by the Castro government in the assassination of JFK, but this hardly eliminated the possibility that Oswald had gone after Kennedy on his own, as a kind of self-appointed lone avenger for America's crimes against Fidel. Indeed, the Lone Avenger scenario simply provided the Warren Report's Lone Gunman point of view a motive the Warren Commission had not claimed for itself. This revised perspective was first advocated by author Albert H. Newman, whose 1970 publication *The Assassination of John F. Kennedy: The Reasons Why* remains one of the most deft presentations of the Lone Avenger scenario. This new point of view was adopted by the courageous investigative reporter Daniel Schorr in his 1977 autobiography, *Clearing the Air*. Jean Davison would later follow form in her book, *Oswald's Game*. As advocated by these three brilliant critics, the Lone Avenger scenario was certainly one credible way to explain certain aspects of Oswald's always curious and seemingly contradictory behavior.

Another ripple was added to this scenario with the 1978 publication of *Legend: The Secret World of Lee Harvey Oswald*, by *Inquest* author Edward Epstein. In his new book, Epstein advanced ideas mostly provided to him by CIA Chief James Jesus Angleton, who was convinced that Oswald's conversion to Communism was quite sincere, and that, while living in the Soviet Union, the ex-Marine

had been trained by the KGB for the life of a double agent upon returning to the U.S.

Neither Epstein, nor Angleton claimed that the KGB ordered the Kennedy assassination. It was more likely, they believed, that somewhere in Dallas or New Orleans Oswald had spun out of control. Angleton's involvement in this scenario was somewhat astounding. When Soviet defector Yuri Ivanovich Nosenko claimed that he had read Oswald's KGB file, and that there was no mention of his Soviet training, Angleton assumed that Nosenko was merely providing Oswald with a cover. He placed Nosenko under CIA house arrest, and for a period of more than four years left him in mostly solitary confinement.

Epstein and Angleton weren't the only ones to believe in a KGB-derived, "Manchurian Candidate," Oswald scenario. In 1977 English writer and attorney Michael Eddowes published *The Oswald File*. It claimed that the man who returned to the U.S. was really a KGB agent who looked like Oswald. The real Lee Harvey

Oswald had never actually left the Soviet Union. Curiously, the Eddowes scenario eventually found favor with Marina Oswald, who on Oct. 4, 1981, allowed Oswald's body to be exhumed from its grave in Texas's Rose Hill Cemetery. The body was taken to nearby Baylor University where a team of forensic pathologists pronounced that it was indeed Lee Harvey Oswald.

In the aftermath of the Church Report, a number of authors who decidedly did not subscribe to the Lone Avenger story helped fill out the biographical profile of the perplexing Mr. Oswald. When all of these insights were taken into consideration, the portrait that emerged was a study in contradictions that could baffle even the most imaginative novelist. By the time of his death, Lee Harvey Oswald appeared to have experienced more lives than an alley cat in the Vieux Carré. Conspiracy theorists were free to pick any one of these incarnations as the "real" Lee, but they did so at the risk of ignoring everything else that became known about this almost mythically mysterious character. There had never been, it now appeared, a single Lee Harvey Oswald.

The "real" Oswald, the full record suggested, tried on and rejected at least nine distinct identities during the course of his brief twenty-four years.

Kid Oswald, Ward of the Mob

New Orleans is my home. I like the high ceilings and the trees and the French Quarter, and everything about New Orleans.

Lee Harvey Oswald

We owe G. Robert Blakey the credit for developing our best picture of Lee Harvey Oswald's world as a young boy. In the course of directing the House Select Committee on Assassinations in 1979, Blakey uncovered much of the hidden detail concerning Oswald's early life on the streets of New Orleans.

Robert E. Lee Oswald died when his infamous second son, Lee, was still in his mother's womb. The day he is born Lee inherits a second set of parents. His mother's sister Lillian, and her husband Charles "Dutz" Murret, will be there for young Lee through the difficult years of his childhood. "Dutz" will become a surrogate father for the boy.

Dutz Murret is a bookmaker in the New Orleans-based Carlos Marcello crime organization. Marcello is at the time one of the most powerful crime leaders in America. His closest associate is Santos Trafficante, mob overlord of the narcotics and gambling empires of Cuba and Florida. Dutz Murret is, however, no more than a mere foot soldier in the New Orleans wing of this operation.

Still, Dutz is well-connected. After Robert E. Lee's death, Murret introduces his sister-in-law, Marguerite Oswald, to a group of men she will befriend during these trying years. Two of these men, Clem Sehrt and Raoul Sere, are lawyers with alleged connections to the Marcello organization. A third man, Sam Termine—who is particularly close to Dutz—is in fact a chauffeur and a bodyguard for the Bayou Godfather himself. All of these men provide support for Marguerite, and her family. It could be said that in his early years, Lee Harvey Oswald is little more than a ward of the Mob.

Pinkie Lee, Student Marxist

When he went to visit my sister, all she said she saw him read was comic books, and this is what she said to the Warren Commission. Well that was true, he did like comic books. Isn't that normal in a young boy?

Marguerite Oswald (as told to Jean Stafford)

Lee Harvey Oswald's early life is anything but stable. When his mother remarries, and is then divorced, young Lee spends his time bouncing back and forth between relatives' homes in Fort Worth and New Orleans. Then, in August of 1952, he rejoins his mother in their new home in the Bronx. At first Lee seemed to thrive in the Big City. His very first year he is elected President of his eighth-grade class at Public School 44 in the Bronx.

The Nine Lives of Ozzie the Rabbit

And then the transformations began. Even at this early date it is possible to detect Oswald's persistent need to erase a new identity at almost the very moment he has actually achieved it. In the Bronx, Lee is walking away from school one day when he is handed a pamphlet on Julius and Ethel Rosenberg published by the local Communist Party. We are led to believe that then and there he becomes an instantaneous convert to the Marxist cause.

A year later, this student body president will be reported to his probation officer for refusing to salute the American flag. His days in student politics are now numbered. He was truant on a regular basis, and spends his time either at the Bronx Zoo, or at home watching television. His favorite program, a family friend will later recall, is *I Lived Three Lives for the FBI*.

Lee Harvey Oswald, Air Patrol Cadet

We are back in New Orleans, and happy to be back. Lee is his old self again after the ordeal in New York.

Marguerite Oswald (Letter to friend, 1955)

Oswald's time in the Bronx is short-lived. In 1954, Marguerite again yanks him out of school, and the two of them move once more back to New Orleans. Lee enrolls in Beauregard Junior High School—his ninth school in 10 years. At Beauregard "Pinkie" renews his enthusiasm for the writings of Karl Marx, and begins to subscribe to a number of Marxist political magazines. Once more, the transformations begin to kick in.

With his schoolmate Edward Voebel, Lee attends afterschool classes sponsored by the local chapter of the Civil Air Patrol. His new cadet leader is none other than right-wing fanatic and young boy fancier, Captain David Ferrie. Under Ferrie's influence, and with the support of the Murret family, Oswald decides to join the Marines.

In fact, Oswald's older brother Robert had already joined the Corps, and this may very well be the impetus for Lee's new interest. Lee Harvey Oswald now memorizes the entire Marine Corps Manual in an effort to enlist prematurely at the age of 16. The Marines reject his application, but the next year, on his 17th birthday, Oswald is accepted as one of The Few, The Proud, The Chosen.

Oswald may be the only 17 year-old boy in America who knows both *Das Kapital* and *The Marine Corps Manual* by heart. The contradictions which will later frustrate and fascinate more than a thousand professional writers and biographers are now readily apparent.

Top Secret Lee, the Marxist Marine

When we were at Atsugi, Lee used to come back to the barracks some times late at night very drunk. He would wake us up by shouting at the top of his lungs: "Save your Confederate money, boys. The South will rise again."

Former Marine Sgt. Gator Daniels

Lee Harvey Oswald joins the Marines on October 24, 1956. He takes his basic training in San Diego, and is then transferred to Camp Pendleton for additional combat training. In San Diego, his inability to hit the side of a barn with his M-1 earns him the endearing nickname "Shitbird" from his fellow Marines. Oswald, however, seems to be thriving in his new identity. He graduates in the top ten of his radar operator class at Kessler Air Force Base in Mississippi. He is given a new nickname, "Ozzie the Rabbit," by his classmates. Lee Harvey Oswald is now considered a *meek* Marxist Marine.

Still spouting Communist propaganda, Oswald is nonetheless assigned to the most sensitive U.S. Intelligence installation in the Pacific, the Atsugi Air Base in Japan. Atsugi is home to the largest CIA station in the region. At Atsugi, the Agency is proceeding with its chemical, biological, and psychological warfare experiments. Atsugi is also home base for a contingent of U-2 reconnaissance planes. These planes will become the central irritant to US/Soviet relations during the decade.

As a radar operator, Oswald works each day inside the high-security "bubble," monitoring the flight patterns of a number of aircraft, including the U-2. A number of Oswald's colleagues at Atsugi assume that Oswald must now be in contact with the CIA on a regular basis.

Oswald's Marxist inclinations, however, are growing ever more apparent. He spends his off-duty hours with Japanese bar girls, and will later claim that he also became involved with a cell of Japanese communists during this period. When Lee's outfit is given orders to ship out for Pacific duties, Oswald shoots himself with his own silver-plated, two-shot derringer to avoid leaving Atsugi. He is shipped out with his squadron anyway, and spends the next five months in the Pacific, with short stops in the Philippines and Corregidor.

When he returns to Atsugi in March, 1958, Oswald is court-martialed for the derringer incident. He is now withdrawn and bitter and he applies for a discharge after his trial. He also picks a fight with one of his supervisors, and is court-martialed a second time. "I've seen enough of a democratic society," he tells a colleague. "When I get out I'm going to try something else."

Oswald is now spending almost all of his off-duty time studying Russian with his new Eurasian girl friend, a woman so beautiful that most of Oswald's Marine buddies consider her way beyond Oswald's league. Oswald's various girlfriends are perhaps Soviet agents, some theorists will later claim. Oswald, some of them maintain, first became a Soviet informer while dancing in their arms.

In November, Oswald is transferred to El Toro Air Base in California. His growing mastery of the Russian language suggests to some researchers that he is now being trained for future assignments by the Office of Naval Intelligence.

In the midst of what writer Philip Melanson has correctly identified as "one of America's most conservative military subcultures," Oswald begins to so loudly trumpet his Marxist leanings that his fellow Marines start calling him "Oswald-skovich." He laughingly replies that he is enjoying his new life as "a Russian spy." This behavior, however, never seems to bother Marine officials, as Oswald, despite a pair of court-martials, will maintain his high-level security clearance until the day he leaves the Marines.

Oswald receives an honorable discharge on September 2, 1959. Although he has a little more than $200 in his bank account, eighteen days later he books passage from New Orleans to his new home in the U.S.S.R.

Comrade Lee Oswald, the Soviet Defector

I affirm that my allegiance is to the Union of Soviet Socialist Republics.

Lee Harvey Oswald (in Moscow)

Keep your nose clean.

Robert Oswald (in a telegram to brother Lee)

By circuitous route, Oswald arrives at the United States Embassy in Moscow on October 31, 1959 to renounce his American citizenship. He is met at the Embassy by diplomat Richard Snyder, who processes his request. Snyder is also in charge of monitoring the Soviet reaction to the U-2 overflights. What with his own U-2 background and information, Oswald should be considered quite a loss for the U.S., and quite a gain for the Soviet Union. Nonetheless, he is released by the U.S. Embassy, and extended a residence visa by the Soviet Union, without ever being debriefed by either the KGB or the CIA.

Oswald is sent to the city of Minsk by Soviet officials. In Minsk he is given a luxury apartment by Soviet standards, a generous stipend by the Red Cross, and he is assigned a rather cushy job in a local radio and television factory. Edward Jay Epstein believes that, in the classic Manchurian Candidate style, the Soviets may have begun to progam Oswald at this time. Outwardly, Oswald seems to be spending his time entertaining good-looking women tourists and leading the life of the new Playboy of Minsk.

Once again, the anticipated moment arrives. In his diary—which Epstein thinks may be a plant—Oswald sows the seeds for his forthcoming repatriation to the United States. "I am starting to reconsider my desire about staying,"he writes in 1960. "The work is drab. The money I get has nowhere to be spent. No nightclubs or bowling alleys. No places of recreation except the trade union dances. I have had enough."

The fact that Gary Powers has crashed his U-2 in the Soviet Union on May 1,

1960, is not even noted in Oswald's writings. Years later, Powers will suggest that it could have been Oswald who provided the Soviets with the information which led to the downing of his flight. At the very least, you would think that Soviet officials would want to talk to Oswald about this. Such a meeting never took place, the Soviets will later say.

A year later, on February 13, 1961, Oswald writes to Richard Snyder, his contact at the U.S. Embassy. He soon reclaims his passport and asks for assistance in returning to the U.S. While waiting for word from Snyder, Oswald marries the attractive Marina Nikolaevna Prusakova at an April ceremony held at the Minsk apartment of her uncle, Colonel Ilya Vasilyevich Prusakov. The Colonel is an official in the Soviet intelligence services. Marina was herself once active in one of the Soviet's most promising youth groups. A month later CIA agent Snyder prevails on the Immigration and Naturalization Service for a special dispensation. On June 1, 1962, Lee Harvey Oswald and his bride leave the Soviet Union for good. The official word from both Moscow and Washington is that, once again, neither the CIA nor the KGB take the time to debrief him, either on departure or arrival.

Texas Ozzie, Among the White Russians

Oswald is his own double.

Don DeLillo

When Lee and Marina arrive on the docks of Hoboken on June 13, 1962, they are met not by the State Department, or the INS, or the FBI. They are met by a representative from Traveler's Aid in New York. The man's name is Spas T. Raiken, and like Marina and Lee, he also has a rather unusual background. As assassination scholar Peter Dale Scott is the first to note, Raiken is at the time the Secretary General of the American Friends of the Anti-Bolshevik Nations Inc., an organization whose politics are somewhere to the right of the old German National Socialist Nazi Party. For reasons that still seem quite uncertain, the two young avowed Marxists are lovingly placed into the warm and friendly hands of the White Russian community of Dallas. If during the early 1960s there is any exile group in America more militant than the anti-Castro Cubans of Miami, Scott says, it would have to be Texas' White Russian community.

Ensconced in Dallas, the Oswalds are a source of great fuss for their new White Russian friends. Among the members of this community, the Oswalds are most closely befriended—some would say *handled*—by a former Polish cavalry officer and Nazi spy by the name of George de Mohrenschildt. "Von" Mohrenschildt, as they would say in the old country, is a real piece of work. During the war, he joined the Nazi cause to help overthrow the forces of Josef Stalin. After the war, like a number of his Nazi colleagues, he

The Nine Lives of Ozzie the Rabbit

became a part of a network of ex-Nazis the CIA would employ to keep Stalin's revolution pinned down in Eastern Europe. Eventually, the Baron wandered west, hooking up finally with a host of fellow White Russians involved with the petroleum industry of Texas.

In October of 1962, Oswald goes to work for Jaggars, Chiles and Stovall, a print shop in downtown Dallas that specializes in highly classified government work. At the time of Oswald's employment the company is working for U.S. Army Intelligence on a series of secret maps of the Soviet Union, China and Cuba—just the kind of job you would assign to a big-mouthed Marxist recently returned from a few years with his comrades in Russia.

Oswald's fellow employees mention that the newly repatriated Lee is at least proficient in locating obscure Soviet place-names. Drawn again into the midst of yet another authoritarian sub-culture, it is only a matter of time before Oswald might again be expected to rebel.

Lee Fidelista, Gunman for the Cause

Lee, I am getting ready to write a book on your so-called defection.
Mother, you are not going to write any book.

Marguerite and Lee Oswald (Texas, 1961)

By January, Oswald has grown once again quite open and boisterous about his still dormant Marxist leanings. He renews his subscriptions to all of his favorite Marxist monthlies, and even prints a free poster for *The Militant* from his desk at Jaggars, Chiles and Stovall. It is at this time that Oswald orders his Mannlicher-Carcano from Klein's Sporting Goods in Chicago. It is at this time, as well, that he allegedly takes the famous backyard photo with his favorite magazine and his favorite gun. A clearly confused Marina will later say that this was the period in which her husband went out hunting both General Walker and Richard Nixon. By April, Lee the Fidelista is out on the open road, the one which will lead him to his waiting grave.

His marriage now coming apart at the seams, Oswald is back in New Orleans that April, living with Uncle Dutz at the bookmaker's apartment. In June he is out on the streets passing out leaflets for the Fair Play for Cuba Committee. Located at 544 Camp Street, the Committee has but one local member: Lee Harvey Oswald.

By August, there seems to be a shift of tactics. On August 5, 1963 Oswald shows up at the business of Carlos Bringuier, a close associate of Sergio Arcacha Smith over on Camp Street. Four days before, the FBI had raided the exile base at Lake Ponchartrain. Oswald tells Bringuier that he is a fellow soldier in the cause, and offers to help Bringuier train guerillas for future raids on Castro.

On Saturday, August 10, a fight breaks out—or is it staged?—when Bringuier finds Oswald back on the streets passing out pro-Castro literature. The FBI uses the occasion of the arrest to interview—debrief?—Oswald. The next Saturday, Oswald and Bringuier appear on local radio to debate their differences about Castro. The debate is sponsored by an organization which is also funded from Camp Street. The switches are coming down so quickly now, it is impossible to follow the true movement of the pea.

In September Oswald leaves New Orleans for Mexico City to once again renounce his American citizenship, and proclaim his desire to return to the Soviet Union via Cuba. On September 25, 1963, a man named "Leon," and his two Latin friends attempt to infiltrate an anti-Castro Cuban exile group in Dallas. On September 27, Oswald—or somebody who looks like Oswald, along with two "Latins"—shows up in Mexico City and makes such a demonstration out of his devotion to Castro, and his hatred of Kennedy, that neither the Cuban nor Soviet embassy will grant him an audience. But the ruckus is memorable.

It is almost November. Oswald and his two companions turn around and make their way back toward Dallas.

Big Easy Lee, The Prodigal Son Comes Home

New Orleans is many things—jazz, pot, pirates, Cajuns, Cubans, voodoo, Bourbon Street, broads, gays... You name it...The birthplace of Lee Harvey Oswald has got it... Oswald was a product of New Orleans.

Rosemary James & Jack Wardlaw

In his 1979 book *Conspiracy*, journalist Anthony Summers provides still another slant on Oswald's last days in New Orleans. In this, the best book ever written on the Kennedy assassination, Summers decided to retread the ground which Jim Garrison had first attempted to plow before becoming hopelessly tangled up in the Clay Shaw trial. Focusing on what really had gone down at 544 Camp Street, Summers came upon a rumor that Guy Banister had occasionally employed young men to infiltrate local pro-Castro student groups. Summers persisted until he turned up two brothers, Allen and Daniel Campbell, both ex-Marines, who had worked for Banister in this capacity.

Daniel Campbell told Summers that he had been working at Camp Street on the day of the famous street fight between Oswald and Bringuier, and that hours later Oswald had come back to the Camp Street offices and used Campbell's phone to make a call. Daniel Campbell's story was supported by his brother.

Allen Campbell claimed that he had been with Guy Banister when the two men came upon Oswald passing out pro-Castro leaflets in front of the International Trade Mart. Assuming that Banister would be characteristically furious at such a sight, Allen Campbell was astonished when Guy Banister just smiled at the sight of Oswald working the crowd.

On obtaining this information, Summers doubled backed to Delphine Roberts, who had been Banister's private secretary and lover when the former G-man ruled over the flock at 544 Camp. Roberts confirmed that Oswald had indeed been working for Guy during the summer of 1963. Oswald's Fair Play for Cuba Committee, Roberts said, had been invented by Oswald and Banister one afternoon at the office. Roberts even remembered the day, earlier that summer, when Oswald had first arrived at Camp Street looking for investigative work. Guy would later be quite furious, Roberts told Summers, when he learned that Oswald had mistakenly printed their address on the actual FPCC pamphlets.

LSD Lee, the White Rabbit of New Orleans

Lee no like America. Lee no like Russia. Lee like moon.

Marina Oswald

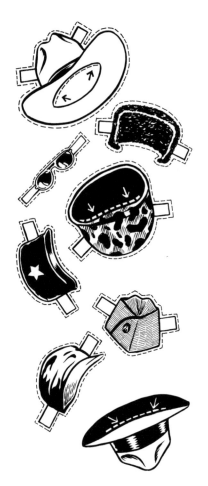

During the course of his very brief life, Lee Harvey Oswald was a street kid with mob connections in New Orleans; the up and coming President of his Junior High School class in the Bronx; a budding Marxist suspended from that class for refusing to salute the American flag; a patriotic Air Patrol Cadet in David Ferrie's private Air Force whose life's goal now was to join the Marines; a top secret Marine radar operator who worked on the U-2; a disenchanted Jarhead who spent his time spouting Marxist slogans to mysterious women companions in expensive Japanese bars; a young ONI agent who underwent language training in California prepatory to going underground in Russia; a Soviet defector treated like royalty by the Soviet officials, his uncle, his wife, and the KGB; a repatriated American welcomed with open arms by the neo-nazi White Russian community of Dallas, Texas; a reborn militant activist who openly proclaimed his support for Castro, while at the same time being secretly connected with one of the most vicious, anti-Castro paramilitary forces in the USA; and, finally, either the chief protagonist, or only a mere patsy, in the assassination of John Fitzgerald Kennedy. There appears to never have been one single Oswald. Rather, he seemed to preside over a number of different personalities, each one threatening to pull him apart at the seams. Psychologically speaking, Oswald does not appear to have been all that stable a fellow.

One final portrait of Lee Harvey Oswald has been given to us by Martin Lee, Jeff Cohen, and the late Robert Ranftel. This pioneering trio of research journalists were the first to draw attention to the strange visitor who appeared before New Orleans assistant district attorney Edward Gillen one afternoon in October, 1963. Gillen offered the man a seat, but the visitor insisted on standing. He wanted to know what the assistant district attorney knew about the legality of importing into the United States a new wonder drug called LSD.

The man claimed to be a serious student of Aldous Huxley's *The Doors of Perception*, and felt that this new drug had the potential for launching a social revolution which could last at least two hundred years. The man also had a source for the drug, and wondered if it would be legal to sell it. In 1963, the only known source for LSD was the Central Intelligence Agency of the USA. The Agency had begun to experiment with acid during the course of Project ARTICHOKE—the CIA's first "Manchurian Candidate" program—back in 1951. The CIA had continued these experiments at two overseas stations into the early 1960's. One of these overseas stations was the Atsugi Air Base in Japan where the Agency regularly fed mescaline, sodium pentathol, downers, speed, and LSD to local bar-hopping, off-duty U.S. Marines.

Ranftel and his associates tracked down one of these Marines. "It was pretty weird," the former Leatherneck said. "I'm eighteen at the time, and chasing all the whores in town, and these CIA guys are buying my drinks and paying for the whores and giving me a whole lot of drinks with lots of weird drugs in them.

"Pretty soon all the shadows are moving around—we're in this bar, see—and Samurais are everywhere, and I started to see skeletons and things. My mind just started boiling over, going about a thousand miles a minute.

"I'm sure there are going to be some little old ladies who're gonna be suprised that illegal drugs like heroin and LSD were freely used by government agents. But," the former Jarhead concluded, "that's just the way it was."

Assistant District Attorney Gillen had no idea, of course, of this secret history on that unusual afternoon in October, 1963. He dismissed the man as a harmless crank.

Watching television the day after President Kennedy's assassination, Gillen was startled to recognize that the man who had been arrested for JFK's murder was in fact the same man who had visited him a month earlier. LSD Lee, the White Rabbit of New Orleans? Well, as Bob Ranftel used to say, it would at least explain Oswald's always curious little smile.

The Nine Lives of Ozzie the Rabbit

With a Little Help from His Friends

The Jack Ruby Mob Boss Controversy

I t is hard to underestimate the impact of the Church Committee Report upon the history of JFK assassination literature. With the release of the report in 1976, the government itself acknowledged that throughout the Kennedy years, the CIA had continued to work with both the Mob and the Cuban exile community in conducting its secret war against Castro. Although the Kennedy brothers had gone out of their way to distance themselves from these associations after the Cuban Missile Crisis, it was nonetheless true that, with Mob support, Cuban exile paramilitaries had continued their raids and the Agency had continued its programmed assassination attempts against Castro, right up until the moment of John Kennedy's death. Unknown to either of the Kennedy brothers, CIA Chief of Special Affairs Desmond Fitzgerald was meeting with AM/LASH in Paris on the day the President was shot. The Church Committee was responsible for these revelations—revelations that would now stand at the center of the assassination controversy.

After debating the strange and confused politics of Lee Harvey Oswald, the critics next turned their attention to Jack Ruby, initiating a reexamination which would lead to the formal reopening of the U.S. government's official investigation into the death of John F. Kennedy. Ruby's tentative and not-so-tentative contacts with Bay of Pigs mob leaders Sam Giancana, Johnny Roselli, Santos Trafficante and the mysterious Carlos Marcello, would now undergo renewed scrutiny—thanks to the revelations which emerged from the Church hearings.

T HE FIRST IMPORTANT BOOK PUBlished on the Ruby connection was Seth Kantor's 1978 *The Ruby Cover-up*. A Scripps-Howard correspondent who often worked out of Dallas in the early 1960s, Kantor knew the local underworld very well; he had contacts among both the Dallas Police and the local gangsters. Kantor was, in fact, an acquaintance of Jack Ruby, with whom he crossed paths several times during the chaos following Kennedy's assassination. They'd bumped into each other at Parkland Hospital immediately after the shooting, Kantor testified to the Warren Commission (an intriguing incident left unexplored). Kantor later spoke with Ruby at the

Henry Wade press conference, in which Ruby obligingly corrected Wade when the DA misstated the name of the Fair Play for Cuba Committee. Kantor had also been in the police department basement when Ruby shot Oswald.

As Kantor pointed out, even the Warren Commission acknowledged that Jack Ruby was a product of the Chicago mob underworld. As a teenager, Jacob "Sparky" Rubinstein and his friend Beryl David Rossofsky (who'd become the great welterweight boxing champion Barney Ross) had run errands for the legendary Al Capone. After arriving in Dallas in 1947, Ruby maintained business ties with the boys back home. He remained particularly tight with Jimmy Weisberg and Paul "Neddle-Nose" Labriola, two Giancana gunmen who would later be victims of one of Chicago's most grisly gangland slayings. Their bodies would be found stuffed in the trunk of a car with their heads chopped off.

Ruby also had friends among the Johnny Roselli mob in Las Vegas and the Mickey Cohen gang in Hollywood. One of Ruby's favorite strip dancers was Juanita Slusher Dale Phillips Sahakian, who became engaged to Cohen while out on bail, appealing a marijuana conviction in Dallas. Mickey's better half was also associated with Pete Marcello's Sho-Bar in New Orleans. The future Mrs. Cohen was better known in strip joints and porno theaters across the Southwest by her stage name: Candy Barr.

The government figured that if anyone could reveal the true nature of Jack Ruby's mob connections it would be Giancana and Roselli. (Ruby had died years earlier of cancer, while awaiting execution in Dallas.) Unfortunately, just before he was to testify at the House Select Committee hearings, Giancana was shot and killed while cooking dinner in his basement apartment in Chicago. At about the same time, Roselli—who had already upset the Mob by leaking details about the Bay of Pigs to Jack Anderson—was fed to the fishes off the coast of Florida.

Roselli's body was discovered in a rusting oil drum that had floated ashore near Miami. He had been shot or stabbed in the stomach; his torso had been hacked open; his legs had been cut off at the thighs and stuffed inside the drum alongside what was left of him. Coroners listed the cause of death as asphyxiation, meaning Roselli was still alive when stuffed in the drum.

The perpetrators of these types of "hits" were the kind of men Jack Ruby had associated with all his life. As Seth Kantor pointed out, in Ruby's world the guilty never faced trial, as key witnesses were regularly eliminated before they ever got a chance to talk.

Jimmy Hoffa was another background figure in Ruby's life who suffered a similiar fate. Days prior to the Kennedy assassination, Ruby was in contact with at least two high-level members of Hoffa's inner circle—Hoffa bodyguard Barney Barker, and regional representative Murray "Dusty" Miller—who would later serve as George Bush's labor coordinator in the future President's unsuccessful 1970 Texas senatorial campaign. As Jack was flat broke and facing labor problems of his own at his club in the fall of 1963, he may simply have been seeking aid and advice from his Teamster friends. The House Select Committee concluded, however, that it was other, more sinister matters, that Ruby needed to discuss with his Teamster pals. Or perhaps the Teamster leaders had other, more sinister matters, they needed to discuss with him? The House Committee never got the chance to ask Hoffa these questions. By the time the Committee began its public hearings, the remains of Mr. Hoffa had already been placed, according to reliable Mob sources, in an end zone grave at the Meadowlands stadium then under construction in New Jersey.

The mob bosses that Jack Ruby was most closely associated with were Santos Trafficante and Trafficante's closest associate, Carlos Marcello of New Orleans. At the time, the two Sicilians controlled the mob's narcotics and gambling empire throughout

With a Little Help from His Friends

the American southeast.

When selecting strippers for his club, Ruby regularly recruited women from Louisiana sex clubs under Marcello's control. Three weeks before the assassination, Ruby called Nofio Pecora, one of Marcello's most trusted lieutenants, in New Orleans. Ruby may have been trying to reach Harold Tannenbaum, a New Orleans club owner, who was then using Pecora's phone. Tannenbaum's club was also in the Marcello orbit. Either way, Ruby's call went directly into the heart of Marcello's crime network.

Jack Ruby did not, however, have to go all the way to New Orleans to feel the presence of Carlos Marcello. Marcello controlled the gambling and narcotics action in Dallas, as well. One of Marcelllo's closest associates, Joe Campisi, ran the Texas rackets for Marcello, and was among the first to visit Ruby in jail after Sparky had been arrested.

Ruby's most significant relationship with the Mob probably came in 1959, when he was allegedly running guns into Cuba for Trafficante. Ruby's contacts at the time included pilot Eddie Browder, and Havana gambler Norman "Roughhouse" Rothman, who ran the San Souci Casino and controlled the slot machines at the Tropicana for Santos Trafficante. Ruby's closest mobster friend, Lewis McWillie, worked for both Rothman and Trafficante at the Tropicana during this pre-Castro period.

After the revolution, Castro threw Trafficante in jail. Trafficante was bewildered and enraged by this—like most successful mob leaders, he had made money arming both Castro's forces and Batista's militia. Placed in the minimum security prison at Trescornia by the ungrateful Fidel, Trafficante was visited by Bay of Pigs co-conspirators Johnny Roselli and Sam Giancana. According to British journalist John Wilson, Trafficante also received a visit from Jack Ruby while at Trescornia. Ruby was in and out of Cuba so often during this period that the House Select Committee concluded that Sparky was probably working as a courier for the Trafficante mob.

Having learned from his mob mentors how to always play both ends against the middle, Ruby was good friends to the cops and the crooks. He was, it's now known, also informing for the FBI in 1959, and maintained a private safe-deposit box which he opened and closed regularly before and after his many visits to Cuba.

The late Johnny Roselli had been right all along. As Roselli had told Jack Anderson, Ruby was just the kind of loyal foot soldier the Mob called on the spur of the moment to go blow somebody's brains out. Thanks to all his friends in the Dallas mob underworld, and in the Dallas police department—Jack Ruby was the ideal candidate to make sure Oswald kept his mouth shut for good.

Jack Ruby's Girls' Theory

Asked why he had killed Oswald, Ruby explained that he didn't want Mrs. Kennedy to have to return to Dallas and suffer the experience of a court trial. That rationale, it was later learned, had been supplied to Ruby by his first lawyer, Tom Howard. But the explanation made sense to some. "That's just like Jack," Carousel Club stripper Diana Hunter said at the time. "He always looked after his dancers first," she said, adding that "for one brief moment—in Jack's eyes—Jacqueline Kennedy must have become one of Jack Ruby's girls."

Tombstone Politics

In the aftermath of the JFK and Oswald assassinations, Penn Jones, Jr., editor and publisher of the tiny *Midlothian* (Texas) *Mirror*, noticed a rather unusual pattern developing concerning witnesses who claimed to have information about the curious criminal background of Mr. Jack Ruby. Many of them, Penn Jones noted, were dropping like flies.

In January of 1964, **Warren Reynolds**, who had witnessed the escape of Tippit's killer, was shot in the head. Reynolds eventually recovered, but in February, 1964, **Betty M. McDonald**, who had offered an alibi for a suspect in the Reynolds shooting, and who had once danced for Jack Ruby, hung herself in a Dallas jail cell.

In March, **Hank Killam**, who was married to one of Jack Ruby's dancers, and who was close friends with a man who once roomed with Lee Harvey Oswald, mysteriously fell from a roof through a plate glass window, and died from a cut throat. In April, **Bill Hunter**, a reporter who had been in Jack Ruby's apartment the day after the assassination, was killed by a gunshot wound.

In August, **Teresa Norton**, another of Ruby's dancers, was shot to death in a local motel. In September, **Jim Koethe**, another reporter who had visited Ruby's apartment with the now-departed Bill Hunter, was killed by a karate chop to his neck.

By 1979, PENN JONES' LIST HAD grown into the size of a small encyclopedia. In addition to Roselli, Giancana, and Hoffa, some of the other people connected to Ruby who suffered violent or mysterious deaths included:

Carlos Marcello associate **David Ferrie**, a victim of a drug overdose in New Orleans in 1967. On the eve of the assassination Ferrie had placed a phone call to Jean West's apartment in Chicago. West, however, was in Dallas with her boyfriend, Lawrence Meyers. That evening Meyers and West were visited by Meyers' old Chicago pal, Jack Ruby.

Eladio del Valle, a prominent Florida Cuban exile leader, and an associate of David Ferrie, was shot in the heart at point-blank range and had his head split open by an axe, only a few hours after Ferrie's death.

Hoffa bodyguard **Dave Yaras**, who was an old friend of Ruby's and a man deeply involved in the Cuban adventure, was murdered in 1974.

George de Mohrenschildt,

Oswald's "advisor," had, like Ruby, been involved in the secret war against Cuba. He was found shot dead in March 1977, not long after being called to testify to the House Select Committee.

Carlos Prio, the former President of Cuba—linked with both Jack Ruby and Frank Sturgis in testimony—was found shot dead a week after the death of George de Mohrenschildt.

Charles Nicoletti, an old Chicago hand also involved in Cuba, was found in a car in a Chicago parking lot with three bullet holes in the back of his head. The House Committee had contacted him the previous day.

William Sullivan, one of J. Edgar Hoover's top aides, and the director of Division Five—which handled the Ruby and Oswald investigations for the Bureau—was shot to death, reportedly in a hunting accident, in 1977.

William Pawley, who collaborated with Mafia figure John Martino in one of the Cuban invasion attempts, apparently shot and killed himself at the time of the House Select Committee hearings, as well.

Means, Motives, and Opportunities

The House Select Committee Controversy (I)

On February 19, 1975, Representative Henry Gonzalez of Texas introduced a bill calling for a Congressional investigation into the deaths of John and Robert Kennedy, and Dr. Martin Luther King. Gonzalez was further inspired by the revelations of the Church Committee Report. The first public showing of the Zapruder film on national television, in 1975, also added public pressure. Finally, on October 17, 1976, the House of Representatives approved the bill, and appointed its own Select Committee on Assassinations to probe domestic assassinations in the same manner the Church Committee had explored plots against foreign leaders.

Those who had pursued the JFK assassination trail for years felt vindicated. The government was re-opening the case; the Warren Report was now officially deemed inadequate.

But the Select Committee ran into controversy right out of the gate—when it named attorney Richard A. Sprague as its chief counsel. This appointment caused great alarm in the critical community. In Philadelphia, Sprague had served as first assistant to Arlen Specter, developer of the single bullet theory. Sprague wasn't the problem, however. Internal bickering over procedural matters and the direction the investigation was to take almost derailed the whole

project. It wasn't until Rep. Lewis Stokes of Ohio was selected as the new chairman, and law professor G. Robert Blakey replaced Sprague that work finally got underway. Critics credit the Congressional Black Caucus with supplying the political muscle that finally got the new investigation off the ground.

REGULAR CLOSED-DOOR MEETINGS BEGAN IN the summer of 1977. By September, 1978, the committee was prepared for public hearings on the JFK murder. On July 29, 1979, the House Select Committee on Assassinations published its final report. The primary conclusions were as follows:

The Warren Commission had been almost entirely correct in its original reconstruction of the actual assassination. The House Committee had employed a battery of scientists to examine each controversial aspect of the Warren Report, and the results of these new tests persuaded the majority of committee members that the Commission had been correct on almost each point. Lee Harvey Oswald had fired three shots at President Kennedy, and one of those bullets had passed through the President to wound Governor Connally. Arlen Specter had been correct. The "magic bullet" theory was substantiated.

Where the Warren Commission had gone wrong—through no fault of its own, the Committee stated—was on the matter of a fourth bullet. Based on acoustical evidence which the Committee had uncovered—a microphone on one of the police escort motorcycles had been left open, producing a dictabelt recording of the actual shooting—the House Committee concluded that a second assassin had fired a fourth shot from the back of the grassy knoll. The President of the United States had in fact been killed by a conspiracy involving at least two shooters, the Select Committee announced.

THE IDENTITY OF THIS SECOND gunman remained a mystery, however. In a carefully worded statement, the committee said that the available evidence did not "preclude the possibility" that individual members of certain anti-Castro groups, or individual members of the Mob may have been involved. The Committee, however, did rule out the possibility that either Oswald, or his unknown associate, had been working on instructions from either Castro, or the KGB.

Turning the entire Report over to the Justice Department, the committee urged Justice to take a new and hard look at the two leading suspects behind the Kennedy assassination: Santos Trafficante and Carlos Marcello.

In what would become one of its most hotly-contested conclusions, the House committee also ruled out the possibility that any official

G. Robert Blakey

agencies—from the Dallas police to the CIA—had played any active role in the murder.

WHAT IS TRULY FASCINATING IS HOW PRECIOUS little attention was paid to this Report in the public press. The *New York Times* was derisive and sly in its response. "To the lay public," the *Times* editorialized on January 7, 1979, "the word [conspiracy] is [usually] freighted with dark connotations of malevolence perpetrated by enemies, foreign and political. But [in this instance] 'two maniacs instead of one' might be more like it."

The *Washington Post* was derisive and angry, suggesting what the Justice Department might now do with the bombshell that had been placed on its desks. "The finding," the *Post* editorialized on January 6, 1979, "appears to be based solely on scientific, acoustical evidence. All that is left is a theory of conspiracy stripped of the international or domestic intrigue on which many of the Warren Commission critics have focused...There seems little reason for the Justice Department to use its resources exploring the dead ends and pursuing the cold trails that the committee is presenting it in the Kennedy case... Leave the matter where it now rests: as one of history's most agonizing unresolved mysteries."

The next day, *Washington Post* columnist Richard Cohen added: "This is... a conspiracy between Lee Harvey Oswald and someone like him—Oswald Harvey Lee. Make up a name. It's a clone of the same man."

Means, Motives and Opportunities

Congress Declares A Conspiracy

The House Select Committee Controversy (II)

How the House Select Committee discovered a fourth shot, and a second assassin, is a story worth telling in more detail.

On Saturday morning, September 17, 1977, Professor Robert Blakey, the newly appointed Chief Counsel of the House Select Committee on Assassinations, hosted a rather unusual meeting in Room 3618 of the House Annex No. 2 Building in Washington, D.C. Joining Blakey in private conference that morning were nine of the Warren Report's most persistent critics. Josiah Thompson, Paul Hoch and Peter Dale Scott had flown in from California. Larry Harris, J. Gary Shaw and Mary Ferrell had come up from Dallas. Sylvia Meagher had arrived from New York City. And Jim Kostman and Kathy Kinsella had joined the rest of their colleagues from the newly formed Assassination Information Bureau in D.C. The "Buffs" were being made welcome at last at the Capitol.

The first day belonged almost entirely to the critics. Blakey asked the critics to tell him where they would recommend he focus the new investigation and the critics most happily complied. At the end of that first day, Mary Ferrell, the Dallas-based critic whose research abilities are considered legend by her colleagues, turned over to Blakey a copy of a Dallas police department dispatch tape which she suggested he might want to hear. The microphone of one of the escort police motorcycles had been left on, and at the exact moment of the assassination, the dispatch tape recorded the sounds of the shooting. Listen very closely, Ferrell told Blakey, and I think you will hear at least four shots.

Blakey realized instantly, of course, what Ferrell was telling him. Using a Mannlicher-Carcano rifle, a lone gunman would only have had time to get off three shots—three, and three only. A fourth shot would require a second gunman. A fourth shot, in short, would require conspiracy.

Blakey had no recourse but to take Mary Ferrell's tape quite seriously. The chief counsel's first job was to find the original of this tape. In short order, the tape was found in the possession of Paul McCaghren, a retired officer who had formerly headed up the Intelligence wing of the the Dallas Police Department. McCaghren had removed the tape from the department for fear it might get lost. The tape, and its supporting materials, were logged in as part of the Committee's files.

Blakey's next step was to seek an independent, preliminary analysis of the contents. He sent the tape to Dr. James Barger, of the firm Bolt, Beranek and Newman, Inc., located in Cambridge, Massachusetts. BBN was the firm chosen by Judge John Sirica to examine the infamous "18 minute gap" tape during the Watergate case. Blakey requested that Barger first determine if any gunshots at all had been recorded.

On July 13, 1978, Dr. Barger called the Chief Counsel in Washington. The scientist said he felt a little sick to his stomach, and strangely embarrassed. Upon analysis, he was forced to report that the tape had recorded the sounds of three to five gunshots. Based on this finding, Barger would now recommend further and more elaborate tests.

On August 20, Blakey and Barger met in Dealey Plaza to attempt an acoustical reconstruction of the shootings. As Blakey would later write in his book, *The Plot to Kill the President*, "for five hours, Barger, his staff and ours, and the Dallas police, orchestrated a slow drum roll of fifty-seven gunshots that broke the still of the morning, each slamming harmlessly into sandbags and echoing into an array of microphones spotted along the path of the 1963 motorcade." Care was taken to insure that the acoustic environment was identical to the circumstances which had prevailed at noontime on Nov. 22, 1963.

Less than a month later, on Sept. 12, 1978, Dr. Barger appeared before the House Committee to discuss his findings. Based on 2,592 calculations, involving 432 combinations of rifle shots and microphone locations, he was now prepared to state that four shots had rung out that noontime in Dallas. Moreover, with a probability factor of 87.5%, three of those shots had been fired from the general direction of the Texas School Book Depository. With a

The "Penguin Strikes Fear In the Heart of Gotham" Conspiracy Theory

Critic Robert Cutler observed that, at the time the President's limousine entered Dealey Plaza, a man had stood on the north side of the Elm street sidewalk, opening and closing an umbrella. This man, Cutler theorized, was one of the President's killers. His umbrella was actually a sophisticated kind of blow gun. In opening and closing the weapon, he was in fact firing poison darts in the President's direction. Cutler was not deterred when the man, Louis Witt, later explained to the House Committee that he had brought the umbrella as a protest to symbolize Neville Chamberlain's appeasement policies in Europe which, he believed, the President's father had once shared.

probability factor of only 50%, a fourth shot had likely been fired from the grassy knoll. Blakey realized immediately that this was not enough. "We had reached the goal line," he would later write, "but we had not scored."

Blakey then went in search of a second opinion. With Barger's help, he turned the evidence over to computer scientists Mark Weiss and Ernest Aschkenasy in New York. The two scientists then developed acoustic "fingerprints" for the grassy knoll shot. On December 18, 1978, Blakey was able to present the full committee the results of tests conducted by Drs. Weiss and Aschkenasy. Like Barger before them, the two men also felt queasy about what they had found.

The grassy knoll shot was there all right. From its fingerprint, the scientists were able to deduce within a margin of error of plus or minus one and a half feet the exact location of the microphone which had recorded the shot. This location corresponded exactly to where the Dallas police had at the time already located the motorcycle in question. The two scientists then reached an even more astounding conclusion. The acoustic fingerprint located the grassy knoll gunman within a margin of error of plus or minus five feet in circumference, at the exact point behind the wooden fence where Lee Bowers had once seen an unidentified man standing, and Sam Holland and his five railroad co-workers, had seen a puff of smoke arise in the seconds after the actual shooting. There was at least one additional shooter working from behind the fence. Josiah Thompson, among others, had been right all along.

Blakey knew instantly what he had, and so did all the other members of the Committee. Blakey had that sinking feeling in his own stomach now; he knew his fate would soon be joined to the cuckoo world where the birds had been singing "conspiracy, conspiracy, conspiracy" for years.

Eleven days later, on December 29, 1978, by a vote of seven to two, the House Select Committee announced these conclusions to an astonished world.

The Cross Talk Problem

Official Washington responded to the central conclusions of the House Select Committee on Assassinations with a good deal of anger, belligerence, and mistrust. Once again, a major advance in the investigation of the murder of John F. Kennedy seemed to create only more divisiveness both within official Washington, and among the critical community.

Blakey sent the Official House Report to the Justice Department, hoping to stir new criminal proceedings. Blakey asked Justice in particular to have its own technical experts re-examine the acoustical evidence, and strongly recommended that Justice ask its criminal division to re-examine the possible involvement of Carlos Marcello and Santos Trafficante.

The Department responded by sitting on the Report until a new Republican administration, headed by Ronald Reagan, took power in the capital. Under Attorney General Ed Meese, the department finally turned the Report over to the National Academy of Scientists, which apparently did not know what to do with it either—until a rock drummer in Ohio responded to an advertisement in a girlie magazine, and basically solved the problem for them.

The drummer's name was Steve Barber, and he had received a copy of the dictabelt tape as a premium in a special Summer 1979 issue of the skin magazine *Gallery*. Playing this tape over and over again, as rock drummers from Ohio who regularly read *Gallery* are apparently wont to do, Barber was able to decode the sound of a human voice on the tape. The voice belonged to Dallas Sheriff Bill Decker, and when it was decoded, Decker could be heard calling in instructions to the force a few minutes after the actual shooting. As Decker's voice could be heard in between the shots, the investigating committee of the National Academy of Scientists hastily decided not to conduct further tests to resolve the overlap inconsistency. They decided instead to reject, out of hand, the authority of the entire Report.

The House Committee, and its experts, stood by their original conclusions, however, and there the matter came to a rest. In such a manner, with the case still wide open, the Kennedy Assassination controversy hobbled into a third decade of future revelations.

Congress Declares a Conspiracy

BOOK FOUR

A Question of Treason

Despite its assertion that JFK was the victim of a conspiracy, the House Select Committee had trouble convincing many people of the accuracy of its verdict. Those who had long defended the Warren Report continued to defend it, while many of those who had long believed in a conspiracy openly criticized the House for failing to implicate certain rogue elements within the CIA for their complicity in the murder.

And so the debate raged on. New twists included conjecture regarding the possible alteration of the President's body enroute from Parkland Hospital in Dallas to Bethesda in Maryland. Intrepid investigative reporters dug deeper along the mob-ridden trails first suggested by the House Report, and produced several books accusing the Mafia of the crime. Finally, in Hollywood, film director Oliver Stone recreated the assassination for a new generation in *JFK*, putting the question of conspiracy back on the front pages.

Stone's film polarized the media and public, and ignited the debate once again.

Perhaps the skeptics were right—the case would never be solved. Yet the critics had accomplished something of enormous value; their criticism had revealed a secret history of the Cold War essential to an understanding of our nation today.

Meanwhile, as darkness and cynicism prevailed, the victim was disinterred, and buried again under a mountain of trash biographies. As the thirtieth anniversary of JFK's death arrived, Americans were challenged to declare how much they still cared about the murdered President. If the concern was there, the case was still open for others to pursue.

31 Cops and Conspirators

The Dallas Police Cover-Up Controversy

With the publication of the House Select Committee on Asssassinations Report, the JFK controversy entered the 1980s. Three distinct points of view had by then emerged from within the critical community. Influenced, in the main, by the writings of Edward Jay Epstein, a first group of critics argued rather convincingly that Oswald's Marxism was both abiding and sincere, and that this pathetic and rootless individual killed JFK at the wishes, and with the assistance, of communist friends in Havana, and possibly even the Soviet Union.

The natural conclusion of this kind of thinking, of course, would be to prompt some right-wing lunatic somewhere to, in retaliation, call for all-out war against Cuba and the USSR. It was the possibility of just this kind of political pressure, these critics argued, that caused the FBI, the CIA, and President Johnson to cover up the "truth" behind the Kennedy killing.

A second corps of critics agreed with Robert Blakey and the House Select Committee. These critics found Jack Ruby a more revealing figure than Lee Harvey Oswald. They believe that the President was murdered at the wishes of at least two powerful Mob leaders, who may have been motivated, in part, by the consistent urging of a powerful Union boss. In typical gangland fashion, these critics stated, Ruby was sent in to seal Oswald's lips forever.

In the fall of 1980, a third point of view came into focus with the publication of Anthony Summer's *Conspiracy*. In his book—an authentic masterpiece of contemporary true crime literature—Summers argued that the plot to kill the President was not limited merely to the Mob, as the House Committee had concluded. The plot also included certain renegade CIA forces who had worked with the Mob on the assassination of Castro—agents who had been responsible in the first instance for the training of the same terrorists who eventually turned their guns on John Kennedy.

Drawing from the insights of Seth Kantor, in *The Ruby Cover Up*, Summers concluded that two overlapping conspiracies surrounded the murder of JFK. The first involved certain rogue CIA agents; the Mob; certain right-wing Cuban paramilitaries; and a very confused individual named Lee Harvey Oswald, ensnared by his own faulty radar into the role of convenient fall guy for the whole operation.

According to Summers, while there was a remote chance that some of the exiles involved were double-agents working for Castro, the weight of the evidence clearly suggested that anti-Communist forces were ultimately responsible for the crime.

The second conspiracy fell into place after Oswald's capture. It involved Jack Ruby, the Mob, and the possibility of help from inside the Dallas police department. Indeed, the role of the Dallas Police in the murder of JFK had been a thorn in the side of government investigators for years.

In the spring of 1964, Warren Commission staff lawyers Burt Griffin and Leon Hubert were called off the case in Dallas, after Griffin had heatedly challenged the testimony of Dallas police sergeant Patrick T. Dean, who had been in charge of basement security at the moment Ruby shot Oswald. As Burt Griffin would later state: "I felt all along that the Dallas Police were prepared to lie to us about anything that would get them into trouble, or embarrass them. No question about that."

Nonetheless, the Warren Commission eventually absolved the Dallas police of any role in the crime. Years later, while aware of the writings of critic Seth Kantor and others, Blakey's committee chose not to pursue this direction much further. Accordingly, it was left to Kantor, and to Summers, to point out that:

• even among fellow law enforcement officials, the Dallas Police Department of the early 60's was considered one of the dirtiest police departments in the country;

• the history of bribes in the department went back at least as far as the 1940's when the Chicago mob, and Jack Ruby, first bought their way into the narcotics, gambling and prostitution action in Dallas;

The Nervous Lover Theory

In the aftermath of the assassination, certain conspiracy theorists speculated that officer J.D. Tippit may have been assigned to shoot and kill Oswald, and was killed by Oswald instead in a spontaneous act of self-defense. According to Dallas critic Larry Harris there might, however, have been a better explanation for Tippit's strange behavior. It seems that at the time Tippit—who was married with three children—was having a wild affair with a waitress at Austin's Barbecue Drive-In. On the morning of November 22, 1963, Tippit's affair was in the course of unravelling—no doubt adding to the erratic behavior he exhibited in front of his colleagues on the fatal day.

• not only did Sergeant Dean and Jack Ruby know each other—both men were known to be occasional dinner guests of local mobster Joe Civello, who represented the interests of Carlos Marcello in Texas;

• evidence indicated Ruby entered the basement, not by the ramp, but by a side alley door, after receiving a call from an officer inside the building that Oswald was about to be moved;

• while in the basement, Ruby's body had been shielded by Sgt. Dean's close associate, officer William "Blackie" Harrison—until the moment Ruby jumped from behind Harrison into Oswald's path,

and shot him in the stomach.

• And finally, both Summers and Kantor felt that Ruby could have been recruited to make the hit during the course of conversations with any one of a number of Hoffa and Marcello henchmen with whom he talked, either in person or on the phone, during the course of that long, awful weekend.

While U.S. goverment investigators seemed determined to give the subject a wide berth, a second conspiracy involving Ruby, certain members of the Dallas police, and the Mob, remained a possibility no open-minded critic could fully ignore.

Blue Spooks in the Machine

In 1981, critic Philip Melanson received a series of documents via the Freedom of Information Act which raised still more questions concerning the role of the CIA inside various American police departments in the 1960's.

While the CIA's own charter forbade the Agency domestic "police or subpoena" power, the Agency had nevertheless been able to wedge itself into domestic affairs by training America's police in the gentle arts of bugging, clandestine action, disguise techniques, lockpicking, and explosives.

To this very day, the Agency continues to conduct similiar programs for the police and security forces of a number of friendly third-world countries.

In return for these services, various police departments would sometimes turn over to the Agency police badges which allowed the CIA to employ its own

agents, posing as cops, within the police departments of a number of major American cities. CIA agents used these badges, ostensibly, to tail "foreign intelligence targets," in the course of their normal breaking and entering activities.

It was also known that the Agency had enjoyed these special privileges in Dallas as late as 1967, when the CIA was in the business of harassing various domestic peace organizations. The documents which Melanson obtained were not nearly as clear about Dallas in the early 1960s, however. In fact, the Dallas records were

strangely absent from these files. In the early 1960s, the files indicated that, during the course of Operation Mongoose, CIA "training" programs were underway in New York, San Francisco, Los Angeles, Chicago, Boston, Philadelphia, Baltimore, Washington D.C., Long Beach, San Diego, Richmond (Virginia), Bloomington (Minnesota), and Miami.

While Dallas was not mentioned as benefiting from such training, Melanson did note that Earl Cabell was Mayor in Dallas at that time. Earl Cabell's brother, Major General Charles Cabell, was one of CIA Director Allen Dulles's most trusted associates. Both men had been fired by President Kennedy after the Bay of Pigs.

It seemed unlikely, Melanson commented, that Mayor Cabell would not be informed about the advantages of such a program by his own brother, who ran these very operations from his desk at CIA.

Shell Games

The CIA/FBI Cover-Up Controversy

In still another controversial area of its report, the House Select Committee joined the Warren Commission in concluding that "the Federal Bureau of Investigation, and Central Intelligence Agency were not involved in the assassination of President Kennedy." In *Conspiracy*, Anthony Summers argued that this particular conclusion was far too tightly drawn. While neither government department may have formally been involved in the enactment of the assassination, Summers noted, the same could not be said about the cover-up which immediately followed.

By the time the House Report was released, the critics had grown quite familiar with the details of secret government collusion published in the 1976 and 1977 reports of the Church Committee. One of the reports, entitled "The Investigation of the Assassination of President John F. Kennedy: Performance of the Intelligence Agencies," detailed the hearings which had been conducted on the subject by Church Committee

members, Senator Richard S. Schweiker of Pennsylvania, and Senator Gary Hart of Colorado.

Critics familiar with the Schweiker/Hart Report would now have a hard time reconciling its details and suggestions with those of Mr. Blakey's House Select Committee. After poking in many of the same corners, Schweiker and Hart had concluded that, in response to requests from the Warren Commission, both the FBI and the CIA had tried to steer the investigation in every direction other than Cuba.

J. Edgar Hoover had certainly followed his own considerable curiosities until fully apprised of the truth concerning the role of the Kennedy brothers in the aftermath of the Bay of Pigs. Hoover even had the chutzpah to approach Bobby Kennedy with the news that one of the architects of their secret assassination program, Sam Giancana, was attempting to blackmail the brothers by schtupping one of Jack's more desirable girlfriends. Hoover knew the Kennedy brothers' campaign against Castro was clearly a time-bomb waiting to explode; and yet, as Schweiker and Hart had discovered, the FBI had stonewalled the investigation each time the Commission had come close to cracking open this particular nest of messy truths.

If Hoover's role in this matter could be considered coy, the role of Warren Commissioner Allen Dulles was nothing short of outrageous. Dulles was the chief architect of the original CIA Manchurian Candidate campaign, and had been the man in charge at the Agency when the Cuban alliance between the CIA and the Mob was first hatched. No one in Washington knew where more skeletons were buried than did Allen Dulles. So it is probably no surprise that he sat silent as the Sphinx on the Warren Commission, and never even nodded in the direction of Cuba the few times the Commission almost accidentally bumped into something approximating the truth.

Anthony Summers was certainly not the only critic to realize that the silence over Cuba by both the FBI and the CIA could be read two ways. The first reading was relatively innocent: both Agencies had steered the Warren Commission away from Cuba for fear of international repercussions.

The second reading was positively sinister, but not, unfortunately, beyond the cover of madness which apparently engulfed this era. One of the reasons the CIA had stayed mum on Cuba, the evidence suggested, was because some of its own agents may have strayed off the reservation, and helped procure the assassins who actually shot President Kennedy.

WHO WAS MAURICE BISHOP?

Working from a description supplied by Alpha 66 founder Antonio Veciana, a number of critics suspected that Bishop was actually former Mexico CIA officer David Atlee Phillips. Agent Phillips maintained until his death that he was not Bishop, although his resume made him a possible candidate. He was on secret CIA assignment in Havana until 1960; he was coordinator of propaganda for the Bay of Pigs invasion, including all the Cuban exile groups handled by CIA (including Alpha 66), and he was covert action chief in Mexico at the time Oswald was alleged to have been there.

THROUGH THE COURSE OF HIS OWN INTERVIEWS, Anthony Summers learned that the CIA had indeed employed a top-level agent known as Maurice Bishop during the period when Alpha 66 leader Anthony Veciana claimed to have observed Bishop—who was Veciana's own control agent—in the company of Lee Harvey Oswald. Why hadn't the Agency produced Maurice Bishop for the Warren Commission, so the entire country could learn just what Mr. Bishop knew, or didn't know, about the assassination?

The director of the CIA's ZR/RIFLE program, William Harvey,

should also have been called before the Commission. Harvey had recruited his two best known assassins, AM/LASH and QJ/WIN, from, respectively, Castro's Cuba and the Corsican underworld of Marseilles. The leader of the Marseilles underground, Antoine Guerini, was a disciple of Lucky Luciano, and a close associate of Luciano's two most powerful successors, Santos Trafficante and Carlos Marcello. The possible role of QJ/WIN in the death of John Kennedy so piqued Gary Hart's curiosity that the Colorado senator attempted, unsuccessfully, to meet secretly with the French assassin during his trip through Europe in 1975.

If anybody could flesh out this picture, it would have to be William Harvey, who, after all, had run the assassination program. And yet, in spite of Allen Dulles's inside information on these matters, neither Harvey or Bishop's names were mentioned once during the course of the entire Warren Commission investigation.

Maybe Bishop and Harvey had something to say on these matters, and maybe they didn't. But the fact that they were never even asked made it impossible for Robert Blakey, or anyone else, to claim beyond a reasonable doubt that the Federal Bureau of Investigation and the Central Intelligence Agency had not been involved in the assassination of President Kennedy. In spite of the House's conclusion, the possibility that certain rogue CIA agents may have participated in the conspiracy to kill JFK was still very much alive.

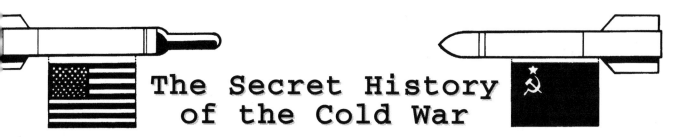

The Secret History of the Cold War

 or most Americans, the news that secret Intelligence forces within their own government had collaborated with Mob gangsters and hitmen to assassinate foreign leaders, and practice various levels of political deceit here at home, came as a more substantial shock than did the news that another American president had been the victim of assassination. The possibility that these activities may have been connected remains a concept that most Americans still have a very hard time trying to swallow.

No one, certainly, has yet proven that the CIA/Mob alliance was directly responsible for the death of President Kennedy. Perhaps no one ever will. But what has emerged after almost thirty years of inquiry into the death of President Kennedy is a picture of secret cold war activities horrid in its intensity.

The secret alliance between the Mob and the Intelligence community began, in the modern era, with Lucky Luciano and the U.S. Navy at the end of World War Two. In 1943, fearful of both Nazi and Italian fascist espionage on the docks of New York, the Navy hired Luciano to be its eyes and ears in the harbor of New York City. Meyer Lansky served as the go-between. Later, Mafia chieftains drew the maps for the Navy prior to the invasion of Sicily. Later still, Mafia bosses—with the agreement of the Navy—took over the political structure of Sicily when Mussolini's own chiefs fell like ten pins under the crush of General Patton's tanks. Luciano was let out of jail immediately after the war for his help in this campaign. Deported back to the newly empowered Sicilian mafia circles, Lucky proceeded to build the largest heroin empire the world had ever seen.

The story, however, was only beginning. In 1947, the newly formed CIA helped to link the Sicilian mafia with the Corsican underworld when it hired a group of Corsican gangsters,

Shell Games

including the legendary "French Connection," to drive the Communist labor unions from the docks of Marseilles. In return, with a blind eye from both the CIA and the DeGaulle government, the Corsicans turned the Marseilles docks into the largest heroin processing center in the Western world. As a result, junkies with needles in their arms began to die in large numbers throughout the United States as pure grade smack began to flow from the south of France through the Lansky/Luciano/Trafficante mob in Toronto and Miami into the streets of the U.S.A.

The renewal of the Mob-Intelligence alliance which took place between the CIA and Mr. Trafficante's friends on the occasion of the Bay of Pigs was mirrored by General DeGaulle's decision to send his own French mob allies into Algeria as counterterrorists to battle his own renegade generals in the OAS. Some of these mobsters, however, found themselves more comfortable with the right-wing generals than they did with DeGaulle, and eventually became a part of a network of right-wing paramilitary activists called the World Anti-Communist League (WACL). The League supplied counterterrorist "death squads" to combat communist insurgency throughout the Third World.

As for the impact of this cancer on the Kennedy assassination, it is known that Guy Banister was a member of the World Anti-Communist

League. A fellow member, and the organization's treasurer, Maurice Brooks Gatlin, is alleged to have delivered a hundred thousand dollars from the Banister/Marcello circle in New Orleans to help the right-wing in France assassinate Charles DeGaulle.

The arms which Banister "lifted" from the depot in Houma, Lousiana belonged to the Schlumberger Corporation, which was owned by a White Russian expatriate in Texas. Schlumberger is alleged to have transported arms for right-wing terrorists in Algiers. One of Jack Ruby's associates,

Thomas Davis, was arrested for running arms to Algiers, and later released through the intervention of QJ/WIN, the former Corsican gunman then under the supervision of William Harvey in the employ of the CIA.

It was Senator Richard Russell who once reportedly said, "Make a list of the world's top one hundred political assassins. Find out if any of them were in Dallas on November 22, 1963. If anyone was, that's your man." Well, one of those assassins was in Dallas on November 22, 1963. He is thought to be Michael Mertz, a Corsican hired gun recruited by DeGaulle to fight in Algiers, who eventually turned cover to fight against DeGaulle with the OAS. Identified by French Intelligence, Mertz was "expelled" into Mexico by U.S. immigration officials just two days after the assassination.

In the hands of INS officials, the Corsican gave his name as Jean Rene Souetre. Souetre was in fact a former OAS officer who had been involved in a number of plots to assassinate Charles de Gaulle. He was allegedly on his way through Dallas to Mexico where still another plot had been prepared to take the life of the visiting French leader. The real Jean Souetre, however, appears to have been in Europe at the time. When asked about these allegations, he told reporters that he was being set up by Mertz, and his Corsican friends, to take the fall.

33 Altered Evidence

The Double Casket Controversy

CLA computer scientist David Lifton became, in 1980, the first critic to seriously investigate the possibility that the conspiracy which killed President John Kennedy went deeper into the interior of secret government planning than anyone had dared to consider.

A brilliant young scientist on his way into a position with John Kennedy's Apollo space program on the day the President was killed, David Lifton built his case on grounds no one had chosen to fully explore before. In his book *Best Evidence*, Lifton returned to the scene of the crime, to Parkland Hospital in particular, in order to chase down a series of clues which would eventually lead to these new openings. Lifton's work in this area was almost entirely original. On its publication, fellow critic Peter Dale Scott would write: Lifton's *Best Evidence* "is the most important new book on the Kennedy

assassination to appear in 14 years."

In *Best Evidence*, Lifton returned to the grounds which Edward Jay Epstein had begun to probe in his 1967 work, *Inquest*. Like Epstein, Lifton also fixed on certain discrepancies in the President's autopsy report. A scientist by disposition and training, Lifton, however, went even further by focusing on the differences between the descriptions of the President's body as it had been examined by eight doctors and five nurses at Parkland Hospital in Dallas, and the official examination authored by Commander Humes after the body arrived at the Bethesda Naval Hospital in Maryland. The descriptions varied to such an extent that the doctors at Parkland and those at Bethesda might just as well have been describing two different bodies—which, in a way, David Lifton suggested they were.

For Lifton, the mystery began with a close reading of the now famous report written by FBI agents James W. Sibert and Francis X. O'Neill. Epstein had made a great deal of the shoulder wound described in that report; its detection had subsequently led the critics to conclude that the official Warren Commission version of the shooting had to be incorrect. Lifton, however, focused on another still aspect of the Sibert/O'Neill report. His attention was captured by two particular paragraphs which had eluded all the other critics up until this time.

"The President's body was removed," Sibert and O'Neill had written, "... and was placed on the autopsy table, at which time the complete body was wrapped in a sheet and the head area contained an additional wrapping which was saturated with blood.

"Following removal of the wrapping," the agents continued, "...it was apparent that a tracheotomy had been performed as well as surgery of the head area, namely, in the top of the skull."

When he first read these paragraphs, Lifton already knew by heart the technical record of what had happened in the emergency room at Parkland. He knew that the Parkland doctors had not performed surgery on the top of the President's head, as described in this report. He knew that no one at Parkland had done any work on the President's head, particularly with a surgical instrument. How could anyone therefore account for the special wrapping, and the apparent surgery the two FBI agents had described after the body had arrived at Bethesda?

Lifton then compared the differences described by the initial medical team who worked on the President's body in Texas, with those described by the examining team at Bethesda.

Eight doctors and five nurses had worked with the President's body at Parkland. In all material respects, their findings were identical. Upon examination, the Parkland team had concluded:

• that the President's throat wound had been one of entry, not exit— meaning, of course, that the bullet had been fired from the front of the limousine;

• that the tracheotomy which they had performed left an incision of no more than two to three centimeters in length;

• that a second wound of no more than five to seven centimeters—or 2-2 3/4 inches—in size had been found on the right-hand side in the back of the skull;

• that this was the only wound of any size found in the President's skull; and

• that no one, among the thirteen member medical staff present, had found any trace whatsoever of still another wound located in the President's back.

The differences between the above description, and those which had emerged from Commander Humes team at Bethesda were simply impossible to reconcile. After performing the official autopsy, the Bethesda team had concluded:

• that the President's throat wound had been one of exit, not entry—meaning, of course, that the shot had been fired from the rear of the limousine;

• that the incision from the Parkland tracheotomy was a good seven to eight centimeters in length;

• that the President's skull wound was four to five times as large as the wound described at Parkland, and extended from the rear of the President's skull forward to his forehead, and

• two puncture wounds of identical size, not detected at Parkland, could now be found in the President's back.

Could either set of descriptions be incorrect? Had either team altered its report to fit a pre-ordained conclusion? Lifton did not think so, even though Commander Humes' testimony before the House Committee left much to be desired. No, Lifton concluded, the Naval Commander and his associates had described the body much as they found it. But so had the staff at Parkland. The solution to the mystery seemed at once both wholly sinister and totally preposterous. What if the President's body had been surgically altered on its flight from Texas to Maryland, Lifton wondered? What if the government itself had altered the "best evidence"—the President's body—in order to hide any trace of more than one assassin?

As paranoid as this seemed, David Lifton's scenario was given further bolstering when he learned from a few members of the Bethesda staff that— separated by a matter of about 47 minutes—two vehicles had pulled up to the hospital that night, both said to be carrying the remains of the dead President. At approximately 6:30 that evening a black Cadillac hearse had arrived at the hospital carrying the President's body. According to two interns who helped unload the contents, the President's body had been placed inside a rubber body bag which had in turn been placed inside a simple gray metal casket.

TRIPLE VISION

From 1963 until 1979, the photographs and x-rays taken of the President's body—particularly of the President's shattered skull—were withheld from the general public by special arrangement with the Kennedy family.

Slowly, however, as a number of critics realized that the President's corpse was, in David Lifton's phrase, the "best evidence" of the crime, the missing photographs and x-rays began to appear.

For David Lifton, the photographic evidence provided still a third lens through which to view the crime. The first lens would be the body as described by the doctors and nurses who had treated it at Parkland Hospital in Dallas. This would be an unaltered view of the President's body as it appeared in the immediate aftermath of the crime. This view, however, differed dramatically from the view which Commander Humes had described in the official autopsy report he authored at the Naval Hospital in Bethesda. In Lifton's view, there was only one explanation: the President's remains had been altered somewhere en route.

In 1979, however, based in part on the efforts of House Select Committee photographic consultant Robert Groden, as well as David Lifton, some original photographs and x-rays were finally made available to citizens studying the crime.

Once again, a mismatch was obtained. In certain critical areas, the x-ray and photographic evidence did not line up with either Dr. Humes' descriptions, or those provided by the staff at Parkland.

In recent years, a debate has broken out between Lifton and Groden as to the reasons why. In his book, *High Treason*, co-authored with Harrison Edward Livingstone, Groden argued that both the photographs and x-rays which were released to the public were out-and-out forgeries, and represented the best evidence we have that the government was itself guilty of "high treason" in its complicity in the murder of JFK.

David Lifton—who seems by far the more careful and original analyst—has taken the alternative position that the Dallas examination records, the Humes autopsy, and the official x-rays and photographs are all honest and faithful depictions of the President's body, but at different stages in the alteration process.

For Lifton, the photos and x-rays provide still a third "lens" through which to view the President's body, as it was "doctored" in the hours after the assassination at the hands of certain complicitous government officials.

From the hard-earned evidence compiled in his book, it is clear, however, that David Lifton also suspects that something like "high treason" is very much at issue in the assassination of John Kennedy.

Under the supervision of "Chief of the Day" Dennis David, seven or eight sailors moved the body to Autopsy a few moments after it arrived.

At 7:17 p.m., the official Naval ambulance said to also be carrying the President's remains arrived at the hospital. The President's wife, Jacqueline, and Attorney General Robert F. Kennedy arrived with this ambulance. So did FBI agents Sibert and O'Neill. The President's body was said to be inside the $4,000 bronze casket which the hospital staff then unloaded for what was, apparently, the second time. Naval Technician J.F. Cutler would remember the moment, exactly. As the President's widow walked through the lobby of the hospital, Cutler looked at her in astonishment. In his hands were x-rays of the President's wounds which had already been taken in the autopsy wing of the hospital in the basement below.

Agents Sibert and O'Neill would attempt to stay with the second casket, but they were separated from it by the Secret Service until approximately 8:00 p.m., when they were finally allowed into the room where Commander Humes' autopsy was already underway. For David Lifton, the suggestion was pretty clear. The second casket had to have been empty all along.

Rejoined with the body, it was at this point in the evening that the FBI agents were able to describe the additional wrapping, saturated with blood, around the head area. It was at this point the two agents noticed that surgery had recently taken place at the top of the skull. But when, exactly, had that surgery taken place?

Neither Lifton, nor anyone else, could take much comfort from the fact that the surgery must have taken place somewhere in that space of time after the body had left Dallas, and before the two FBI Agents were let into the autopsy room at 8:00 p.m. on the evening of November 22, 1963. Someone had secretly operated on the President. Someone had altered his original wounds. David Lifton's *Best Evidence* allowed for no explanation other than this singular and shocking conclusion.

The "What Should I Tell Mr. Khrushchev If He Calls?" Theory

The decision to suddenly whisk JFK's dead body to Naval Headquarters in Maryland for an "official" autopsy was made so rapidly, and with so much consternation among confused federal and local officials arguing over jurisdiction, that the officially designated White House "bagman"—the man entrusted with the Red Phone, used to instantly ignite nuclear retaliation against a foreign foe—was left cooling his heels on the tarmac in Dallas as Lyndon Johnson went winging his way north to his new job in Washington, D.C.

Conspiracy of Silence

34

The Ongoing X-Rays and Autopsy Room Controversy

argely because the general public has no idea what to believe when hard science dominates the course of the JFK assassination debate, David Lifton's *Best Evidence* has existed in a state of limbo since its publication. While the book's scholarship and investigative research has stood the test of critical attention, *Best Evidence* —in spite of its numerous editions—remains to this day a book more respected than read. Lifton's conclusions, however, were reinforced in 1992 by the testimony of Parkland doctor Charles A. Crenshaw, in his own book, *JFK: Conspiracy of Silence*.

On the afternoon of November 22, 1963, Crenshaw was one of the doctors working in the emergency room at Parkland Hospital attempting to save the President's life. For the next twenty-nine years, Crenshaw listened to the great debate concerning the nature of Kennedy's wounds swirl all about him, knowing all the while that he had eyewitness information which would clearly tilt the debate in one particular direction. In spite of what the surgeons in Maryland would claim, and in spite of the Warren Commission which backed up the testimony of the Maryland team, Crenshaw was there, in the Dallas emergency room, and saw the President's body examined first-hand.

Crenshaw knew that the two head wounds he saw — one in the top of the head, the other in the throat — were more or less standard

The AMA Rides To the Rescue

The predictable counterattack against Dr. Crenshaw was launched from the pages of the prestigious *Journal of the American Medical Association*.

It is hopefully not stretching the point too far to claim the pages of *JAMA* are to the American medical establishment what the Decrees of the Papacy are to loyal members of the Roman Church. Egged on by *JAMA* editor George D. Lundberg—who appeared on national television to promote the issue with vindictive glee—the two major surgeons from Bethesda, Commander James Humes and Dr. Thomas Boswell, appeared in the pages of the May 29, 1992 issue of the *Journal* to rake Dr. Crenshaw's claims over the hot coals of established critical scorn.

What the reporters failed to note was the not insignificant fact that Humes and Boswell were the Bethesda doctors, and therefore hadn't the beginning of an idea as to what Crenshaw had seen, or had not seen, in the emergency room at Parkland.

What had happened to the President's remains en route was out of their domain. Realizing this, *JAMA* thus appended to their interview comments from a few selected members of the Parkland staff.

Dr. Perry, who had conducted the tracheostomy at Parkland, told *JAMA* more or less what he had told the Warren Commission: that he was too busy trying to save the President's life to note definitively whether he was dealing with an exit or entry wound in the President's throat. Nothing said in Dallas flatly contradicted anything Crenshaw had said.

entry wounds. "I was standing at about the President's waist," Crenshaw would write of the experience, "making a quick inspection of [President Kennedy's] general appearance. His face was unmarked and exquisite. His eyes were open and divergent. They were still and devoid of life.

"Then I noticed that the entire right hemisphere of his brain was missing," Crenshaw continued, "beginning at his hairline, and extending all the way behind his right ear. Pieces of skull that hadn't been blown away were hanging by his blood-matted hair. Based upon my experience with trauma to the head from gunshots, I knew that only a high-velocity bullet from a rifle could dissect a cranium that way. Part of his brain, the cerebellum, was dangling from the back of his head by a single strand of tissue, looking like a piece of dark gray, blood-soaked sponge that would easily fit in the palm of the hand.

"Blood was still seeping from the wound onto the gurney, dripping into the kick bucket on the floor. Seeing that, I became even more pessimistic. I also identified a small opening about the diameter of a pencil at the midline of his throat to be an entry bullet hole. There was no doubt in my mind about that wound. I had seen dozens of entry wounds in the emergency room. At that point, I knew he had been shot at least twice... I believed, as I think every doctor in Trauma Room 1 [also believed], that the President was dead from the very beginning. But goddammit, he was the President of the United States, and we had to something. After all, we were surgeons."

In a manner which would directly comment upon David Lifton's discoveries, Crenshaw was on hand when the casket from the Oneal Funeral Home was rolled into the Trauma Room to take the President's remains off to Maryland. "I was the only doctor in the room," Crenshaw would later recall. "All of the tubes had been removed from the President, his body had been cleaned, and he had been wrapped in two white sheets. The casket was opened, and two nurses placed a plastic-mattress covering over the white-velvet lining to keep any blood that might still seep from the wounds from staining the material... Four of us [then] lifted the President into the casket and placed his neatly folded clothes at his feet."

When Dr. Crenshaw last saw the President's remains there was no question of body bags. The body was delicately placed inside a velvet-lined casket. The casket was then sealed, and sent off to Maryland. Crenshaw was shocked, therefore, when he later saw the autopsy photographs from Bethesda. "The doctors there had recorded the condition of John F. Kennedy's cranium, a state that had substantially changed during the period of six hours and over a distance of 1,500 miles. Great effort had been made to reconstruct the back of the President's head, and the incision [Dr. Malcolm] Perry had made in his throat at Parkland for the tracheostomy had been enlarged and mangled as if someone had conducted another procedure. It looked to be the work of a butcher," Crenshaw commented... "No doubt, someone had gone to a great deal of trouble to show a different story than we had seen at Parkland."

But why had the doctor waited until 1992 to come forward with his story? "Every doctor in Trauma Room 1 had his own reasons for not publicly refuting the 'official line,'" Crenshaw answered, candidly... "I believe there was a common denominator in our silence—a fearful perception that to come forward with what we believed to be the medical truth would be asking for trouble. Although we never admitted it to one another, we realized that the inertia of the established story was so powerful, so thoroughly presented, so adamantly accepted, that it would bury anyone who stood in its path."

Crenshaw himself waited until his retirement from professional medicine before coming forward with his own memoirs of the day's events.

D AVID LIFTON WAS NOT THE ONLY CRITIC IN 1992 to have his work reinforced by further revelations. On May 28th, Naval X-ray technican Jerrol Custer, and photographer Floyd Riebe came forward to say that both Robert Groden and Harrison Edward Livingstone had been correct in asserting that the publicly released photographs and X-rays of the President's autopsy were as phony as three dollar bills. The two men knew what they were talking about. Custer had taken the X-rays that evening. Riebe had taken the photographs.

Custer noted that the released X-rays showed a black hole where the right side of Kennedy's face should have been. The released X-ray was a fake. Looking at the adjoining photographs, Riebe commented that the released prints had been doctored up "one way or another." As the poet once said, something rotten had gone down in the state of Maryland.

The "Hardest Working Man in Show Business" Theory

By Texas State Law, John Kennedy's autopsy should have been conducted in Dallas. The Secret Service literally had to bowl through Dallas authorities to get the President's remains on the plane, and out of state. One of the men who stood in the way was Dallas Medical Examiner, Dr. Earl Rose. While Rose would have the historicial distinction of being the man who later autopsied Officer Tippit, Lee Harvey Oswald, and ultimately Jack Ruby, he stepped aside that day in Dallas in the face of very determined Secret Service agent Roy H. Kellerman, having decided that being cold-cocked by the Secret Service would do little to enhance an otherwise distinguished medical career.

The Kingfish's Vendetta

The Continuing Carlos Marcello Controversy

When asked what he did for a living, Carlos Marcello liked to tell reporters he sold tomatoes. If this was true, with well over a billion dollars annually flowing through the coffers of his various New Orleans-based operations, Marcello was undoubtedly the most successful tomato salesman in world history.

In the year of John Kennedy's assassination, a New Orleans crime commission estimated that Marcello was annually taking in $500 million from his illegal gambling operations; $100 million from 1, 500 syndicate-connected bars and saloons; $8 million from burglaries and holdups; $6 million from prostitution, and perhaps as much as $400 million from so-called legitimate investments in transportation, finance and housing. The commission didn't venture a guess as to how much additional cash Marcello was raking in from the sale and distribution of narcotics.

A Sicilian born in Tunisia as his parents made their way to America, Marcello was called the "Midas of the Mafia" by some of his more envious contemporaries. Because he stood only five-foot-six in his stockinged feet, Marcello was also called the "Mafia Midget" by people not that anxious to actually cross his path. Marcello's road to fortune was paved by mob leader Frank Costello, who in the 1930's decided to move his slot machines out of New York City,

and relocate the action in the fertile parishes of yonder New Orleans. On his arrival, Frank was welcomed with open arms by Louisiana's controversial senator, Huey B. Long.

AT THE TIME, MARCELLO WAS KNOWN ONLY as a sawed-off killer who had shotgunned his way to power in tribal wars with other ethnic, New Orleans mob dogs. With Costello as an active partner, Marcello's fortunes skyrocketed. In 1947, the extraordinary Meyer Lansky threw his syndicate muscle behind the Costello/Marcello alliance, and the New Orleans rackets grew semi-legitimate: a racetrack wire service, several plush new casinos and, of course, quite a few more slot machines.

As New Orleans' new crime boss, Marcello succeeded Sam Carolla, who in turn had succeeded Charles Montranga, the greatest of all the early New Orleans Mafia leaders. Montranga was a legend. With the scar on his neck to prove it, he was the sole survivor of the 1890 mass vigilante lynching of twenty-two Mafia members, retribution for the killing of New Orleans Police Chief David Hennessey. Carlos Marcello was now a man of history.

By the early 1960s, the penniless immigrant was living a life much like the Roman emperors of old. Carlos owned motels, a towering juke-box, a vending machine company, a lucrative French Quarter

The Dead Dog Theory

When Carlos Marcello uttered his famous death threat against the Kennedys on Churchill Farms, he used a brutal analogy to explain why it made more sense to kill John Kennedy, even though it was his brother Robert who had humiliated Marcello by deporting him to Guatemala. "If you cut off a dog's tail," Marcello is alleged to have said, "the dog will only keep biting. But if you cut off its head, the dog will die."

sightseeing bus company, and a 6, 500 acre, $22 million estate called Churchill Farms, just outside New Orleans in Jefferson Parish. Marcello had by 1962 become the undisputed Mob Boss of a territory which stretched west from Louisiana through Texas.

MARCELLO'S OUTLAW SUCCESS WAS SCRUTI-nized by the 1959 McClellan Committee on organized crime, under the direction of chief counsel Robert Kennedy. Marcello's disdain for Kennedy's crimebuster attitude so enraged the future Attorney General that he vowed to "get" the New Orleans Kingfish. When he discovered that Marcello had never bothered to become a naturalized U.S. citizen, Kennedy arranged for the INS to grab Marcello and unceremoniously deport him. The Kingfish, bereft of baggage and dignity, was dumped in the middle of Guatemala.

Marcello was soon back in the States—according to some reports he was flown back by one of his personal pilots, David Ferrie. One night at Churchill Farms, according to Las Vegas promoter Edward Becker, Marcello exploded when the subject turned to the now-Attorney General. "Don't worry about that little Bobby son-of-a bitch," he shouted, "He's going to be taken care of."

Marcello then described his plan. A loose "nut" would be used for the job, someone who could be controlled, and who would divert attention away from the involvement of the Mob. The actual target, however, would be John, not Bobby, Kennedy (see text box, preceeding page).

Journalist Ed Reid had first written about the Churchill Farms incident in his 1963 book, The Grim Reapers. Robert Blakey would make much of it in the 1979 House Select Committee on Assassinations Report. Both John H. Davis and David Scheim would elaborate even further in their own Mob/JFK books, respectively Mafia Kingfish: Carlos Marcello and the Assassination of John F. Kennedy, and Contract on America: The Mafia Murder of President John F. Kennedy. These two books helped make the "Mob Did It" school of assassination critics grow all the more persuasive during the course of the 1980's.

In 1992 the school received a major contribution from an unexpected source: Jimmy Hoffa and San-tos Trafficante's attorney, Frank Ragano, who was also a close friend of Carlos Marcello. Based on Ragano's conversations with journalist Jack Newfield, the following composite calendar of critical events came into focus:

August, 1962—Teamster boss Jimmy Hoffa talks with associate Ed Partin about possible plans to kill both Robert and John Kennedy.

September, 1962—Carlos Marcello discusses canine etiquette with former Las Vegas operator Edward Becker at his home outside New Orleans.

February, 1963—Jimmy Hoffa sends his lawyer, Frank Ragano, to enlist his two friends, Santos Trafficante and Carlos Marcello, in helping Hoffa get rid of the Kennedy brothers. The way the two mob bosses dance around their response leads Ragano to believe that Jimmy shouldn't worry about a thing—a plan is already underway.

December, 1963—The first time Hoffa sees Ragano after the assassination, Hoffa tells him "I'll never forget what Santos did for me."

February, 1987—Almost twenty-four years later, on the occasion of a reunion between the lawyer and his old client, Trafficante tells Ragano, "Carlos fucked up. We shouldn't have gotten rid of Giovanni. We should have killed Bobby."

THE ONLY BIG QUESTION REMAINING CON-cerned Ragano's credibility. Could he be believed? The chief counsel of the House Committee thought so. "I believe Ragano," Robert Blakey said. "This is the most plausible and logical explanation of the assassination."

Noted crime journalist Nicholas Pileggi also provided strong support. "Ragano is one hundred percent credible," Pileggi added. "He knows."

Even Robert Kennedy's trusted aide Richard Goodwin now had to wonder. "Before he was killed, Bobby came to suspect that his brother had been murdered by 'that mob guy down in New Orleans,'" Goodwin acknowledged.

After thirty years, leading advocates of "The Mob Did It" school of JFK conspiracy thinking had reason to believe that the case was finally moving toward a conclusion.

Of Gods and Goddesses

The Judith Exner/Marilyn Monroe Controversy

During the course of this thirty year-old investigation into the death of JFK, a strange thing happened to the corpse. A new generation of grave robbers, disguised as critics and historians, slipped into the cemetary and exchanged bodies in the dead of night. A man who had died in a far more innocent era as an inspiration to his nation was reborn in our own as a figure of political corruption and moral infidelity. It was as if, unsure of the viability of their case, the critics of the critics suddenly changed course, and decided to haul the legend of the victim back down to earth.

The young man who had died that autumn day in Dallas was, in his time, the very lion's heart of a spirited and invigorated nation. Thirty years later the critics had transformed the legend of John Kennedy into that of a reckless Irish cowboy, controlled only by the surge of his own insatiable sexual desires. In the eyes of his critics, it had become appropriate to think of the once noble Jack Kennedy—in the manner of a racist British novel—as just another "Buck." Reading through a mountain of "trash" JFK biographies, it sometimes felt that this devaluation process was rapidly becoming the most effective cover-up of them all. The inference was that JFK was hardly worth the justice still being sought for him.

In a way, the need for a change was understandable. Thirty years of JFK assassination literature had—if nothing else—managed to expose the darkest secrets of American Cold War political life. It was not as if the Kennedy brothers had not made their own special pacts with the Devil. It was utter nonsense for Kennedy apologists to insist that if Kennedy had only known in time there would never have been a CIA-Mob alliance, a covert warfare policy aimed at a number of Third World countries, or an actual assassination program in which U.S. tax dollars funded murder attempts against selected leaders of certain foreign governments. In one form or another, Jack Kennedy had approved each and every one of these operations. Indeed, it could be argued that Kennedy had, in the end, been killed by the backfire of his own mad and warlike enthusiasms.

B UT WERE THESE REVELATIONS THE REASON that Kennedy's historical reputation had undergone such a major transformation? It did not appear so. Sex is what made the difference.

In 1977, a former Hollywood beauty queen by the name of Judith Campbell Exner first set this process in motion. In her book *My Story*, co-written by true crime expert Ovid Demaris, the author recounts her affair with JFK. While the rumors had always been rampant in Washington, and J. Edgar Hoover had discussed the matter privately with Robert Kennedy, it was Exner who provided the first recorded glimpse of Kennedy's truly legendary sexual trysts and marital infidelities.

The implications of Exner's story were shocking. The well-to-do, and educated Hollywood beauty had been introduced to Kennedy in February of 1960 by none other than Frank Sinatra, whose own history with the mob went back at least as far as 1948, when he had been summoned to Havana to serenade the triumphant return of heroin king—and US Naval Intelligence collaborator—Lucky Luciano.

Exner's story, however, spoke of a triangle. At the time she first climbed into bed with the President, Exner was also having an affair with Sam Giancana, one of the three wise men whom the CIA had asked to kill Castro the year before.

In later retellings of her story Exner would speak of bathing in the next room as Giananca and Kennedy sat on the edge of the bed, money-filled suitcases lying before them, talking of bought elections and burial plans for Castro. Was Campbell Exner simply making this up? Kennedy loyalist Kenny O'Donnell

thought so. "Who is Judith Campbell?" he asked. "The only Campbell I ever knew was chunky vegetable soup."

N EVERTHELESS, IN A NEW AND FAR MORE jaded era, a number of critics did believe Ms. Exner. Indeed, by the mid-1980s, schooled by Watergate, a journalistic majority seemed convinced that our movie-star handsome President had bedded down just about every starlet in Southern California. In a curious way, the Exner story had strangely corroborated—at least in the pop culture psyche—the almost fairy tale-like revelation that JFK had also had an affair with The Goddess, Marilyn Monroe.

The mere suggestion of romance between these two pop culture icons proved irresistably spine-tingling to an easily tittilated nation.

The point was no longer—*Who Killed JFK?* The new critics now asked *Who were these Kennedy boys to play holier than thou? Why, they were just as dirty as their killers.* In such a manner, the new critics were able to diminish the final worth of a life snuffed out at the peak of its promise.

And yet, for those who resisted this devaluation—who remembered the positive qualities of this earlier era—the issue could no longer be one of mere factual detail. JFK had now become legend—and a victim of the politics of legend.

"Over the years, the myth of Jack Kennedy has become Janus-like," writer Art Spiegelman has stated. "In the old religions, the gods were commonly depicted as naughty, ill-tempered, sexually promiscuous. In a way, it was an important part of their Godhead. Depending on the needs of the people who worshipped them, the old Gods regularly grew different, often opposing sides to their personalities over time."

And, that, finally, seemed right. In critic David Talbott's words, John Kennedy had become as much a Prince of Darkness as he had once been a Prince of Light. For those who remembered, the Kennedy controversy now could be forwarded only by folk tales—or, for that matter, by the movies.

Assassination Lit: 101

A number of significant novelists have attempted to measure the impact of JFK's death upon the American imagination. The unsolved murder of this popular President became a theme of American literature almost as quickly as it became a challenge for investigative journalists.

Reviewing Mark Lane's *Rush to Judgment* in 1966, Norman Mailer—who at times in the early 1960s seemed a literary alter-ego (an alter-id?) to the President—discussed the need for a Writers Commission to take on the job the Warren Commission had failed to accomplish. "One would propose one last new commission, one real commission—a literary commission supported by public subscription to spend a few years on the case," Mailer said. "I would trust a commission headed by Edmund Wilson before I trusted another by Earl Warren. Wouldn't you?"

Unfortunately, no one ever got around to appointing members to Mailer's new Wilson Commission. Yet, over the years, more than a few volunteers managed to file their own special reports. Some might argue that the very first Kennedy assassination novel was Richard Condon's *The Manchurian Candidate*, published in 1959. The editors of *The Nation* certainly saw the Lee Harvey Oswald-Raymond Shaw parallels, and—as commented upon in Chapter Two of this book—invited Condon to comment upon the Shaw/Oswald similarities in the December, 1963 issue.

Some of the more interesting novels to follow include Wesley S. Thurston's *The Trumpets of November*, in 1966; Vance Bourjaily's *The Man Who Knew Kennedy*, in 1967;

> **"The Assassination Festival of Jacqueline The Praying Mantis"**
>
> The mantle of "craziest book ever written on the JFK assassination" is perhaps the most hotly contested of all the various canons of JFK Conspiracy Literature. After much contemplation, however, the award seems most properly to belong to Mr. James M. Beasely and Mr. Jerald Lee Cockburn for their 1971 privately printed pamphlet, bearing the above title, in which, based on Jacqueline Kennedy's own testimony, the two San Francisco visionaries conclude that the murder ultimately represented the fulfillment of a century old grudge between the French Bouvier and Irish Kennedy clans!

Harry J. Jones' *The Private Army*, in 1969; Barry N. Malzberg's brilliant science-fiction treatment of the assassination, *The Destruction of the Temple*, in 1974; and Richard Condon's later *Winter Kills*, in which the always thrilling suspense master has his fictional Kennedy character murdered in a plot launched by his own father! *Winter Kills* was published in 1974, at a time when the Church Committee was about to open the sewers of the Cold War, and the country as a whole was about to be drowned in various forms of apocrypha.

Indeed, if it could be said that the Kennedy assassination was the seminal event for a new generation of novelists, then that generation would have to be the punk and post-modern fictionalists. The brilliant J.G. Ballard began to write Kennedy "essays" as early as 1967; Jello Biafra began to write his own "magic bullet music lyrics" for the Dead Kennedys in the early 1980s, and Derek Pell's fascinating collection of prose poems and various mad and inspired ravings, *Assassination Rhapsody*, was first published in 1989 in the wacky *Semiotext(e) Foreign Agents Series*.

Based on a careful reading of the various works of non-fictional literature discussed in this book, Don DeLillo's *Libra* is still perhaps the best "Kennedy assassination" novel. DeLillo's story is so skillfully realized, so brilliantly nuanced, it deserves a prominent place on any list of the best works, factual or fiction, ever written about the murder of JFK. *Libra* creates a mood for the whole assassination era which simply can't be achieved in non-fiction form.

37 Camelot Revisited

The Oliver Stone Controversy

T he JFK assassination reached a new level of public prominence with the December, 1991 release of Oliver Stone's film *JFK*. By the time of its premiere, *JFK* was already mired in controversy in the pages of the popular press. While the film was still being made, the *Washington Post* and *Time* had already launched astounding critical attacks against the movie, based solely on early drafts of the screenplay.

Stone's *JFK* was principally based on Jim Garrison's memoir of his Kennedy investigation, *On The Trail Of the Assassins*, an account which had become a national bestseller upon publication in 1988. Stone's approach to the movie was clearly

pro-Garrison; and so, before the film was even finished, the critics took out their old clip files, and began to beat on all the old war drums once again.

Most of what would be written against the film, either before or after its release, was a restatement of arguments first used against the critics of the original Lone Gunman version of the murder. By now, readers of this book probably know most of those arguments by heart. The majority of the film's critics simply did not understand the intricate details of the case; nor had they been following the cascade of revelations which began in 1965 with the publication of Mark Lane's *Rush to Judgment* and Edward Jay Epstein's *Inquest*, and continued right through the Church Committee and House Select Committee Reports, and the publication of Anthony Summer's book *Conspiracy*. The majority of the criticism, in short, was wildly, and wickedly uninformed.

As a movie, not a political manifesto—as much as it also seemed to want to claim that ground—Stone's *JFK* was compelling cinema. Connecting many of its viewers with long-buried emotions once felt for "our dying King"—even the film's poetry was correctly Arthurian—*JFK* was perhaps most convincing in evoking the shock and sense of betrayal so many had experienced when Kennedy's Camelot was revealed as having too much in common with Al Capone's Chicago.

Certainly, the film was at its best in properly crediting Garrison for a number of his more important contributions. Garrison had been, after all, the first public official in America to insist that John Kennedy had been killed by a conspiracy of political forces. Garrison had also been the first official to focus the nation's attention on that strange aggregation of right-wing lunatics, militant anti-Castro Cubans, and renegade government patriots who had made 544 Camp Street a lethal bunker of fascist paranoia back in the early 1960's.

If one were asked to choose between the integrity of the film and the integrity of its most strident critics, the vote would have to go to Stone and Garrison, hands down. Unfortunately, the choice was not so simple.

IN HIS FILM, OLIVER STONE had doggedly followed Jim Garrison through the very same round of aversions and mistakes that ruined the actual Garrison investigation. Even though it had become known by 1991 that Clay Shaw had worked with the CIA in the early 1950's—advising the Agency on matters of international trade—the film offered no new evidence to prove that Shaw had plotted with Banister and Ferrie to kill John Kennedy. The witnesses who alleged otherwise back in 1969 still seemed like heroin addicts and screwballs in 1991.

The film also reflected the other major flaw in the Garrison investigation. Stone's *JFK* never even hinted at the fact that David Ferrie, Guy Banister, Jack Ruby, and even Lee Harvey Oswald's New Orleans host—good old "Uncle Dutz"—were all connected by a criminal network headquartered in New Orleans under the leadership of Carlos Marcello, one of three men whom the House Select Committee had listed as having the "means, motive and opportunity" to kill President Kennedy. Jim Garrison would, in fact, go to his grave claiming that if there was a crime network in New Orleans, and if a man named Carlos Marcello headed it, that was news to him.

Stone's film also introduced into the mix a new motive for the crime. Upon reading an advance copy of John M. Newman's book *JFK and Vietnam*, based on research first developed by professor Peter Dale Scott in 1971, both Stone and Garrison placed great emphasis on the shift in American policy toward Vietnam which occurred immediately after President Kennedy's death. Prior to his death Kennedy had ordered the initial withdrawal of a thousand military advisors then working in the old French colony in southeast Asia. After JFK's death, Lyndon Johnson reversed direction, and began the escalation process which would make Vietnam the dominant foreign policy issue, and a graveyard for young and patriotic Vietnamese and American soldiers, during the forthcoming decade.

The chain of evidence which might link Lyndon Johnson and his Joint Chief of Staffs, to Clay Shaw and the Camp Street Cabal—or to Carlos Marcello and his friends in the CIA—would be revealed only by conjecture and wildly paranoid assertions in Stone's otherwise dramatic and compelling film.

The Potato Salad Conspiracy Theory

In lambasting Oliver Stone's film *JFK* in the pages of *The Nation*, the acidic Alexander Cockburn smelled an old plot. Stone had first been given a copy of the Garrison book by Ellen Ray, the book's publisher, and the co-publisher of *Covert Action Information Bulletin* and *Lies of Our Times*. Ray is one of those people, Cockburn tells us, who feels that history took a U-turn for the worse after the death of JFK. Perhaps, as Cockburn mockingly states, "we should take a biographical approach and argue that [the germ of the film] goes all the way back to Ellen's Catholic girlhood, with an icon of JFK on the wall." From Cockburn's criticism it seems possible to infer that a) the Plot to Reveal the Plot to Kill JFK was secretly engineered by the Knights of Malta, and b) brother Cockburn's own well-known distaste for potato salad dates back to the days of the Irish Potato Famine.

The Anton Cermak Precedent

Towards the end of *JFK*, Jim Garrison (as portrayed by Kevin Costner) explains why the Mob was never considered a viable culprit during his investigation. "The Mob wouldn't have the guts or the power for something of this magnitude," Garrison concludes. "Assassins need payrolls, orders, times, schedules. This was a military-style ambush from start to finish... a coup d'etat with Lyndon Johnson waiting in the wings." In this scene, as elsewhere in their tale, Garrison and Stone again underestimate the power and ambition of organized crime.

THE TIME WAS 1933, and the target was Chicago's newly-elected mayor, Anton Cermak, who had risen to office by vowing to rid the Windy City of Capone's mob scourge. On February 15, 1933, while visiting in Miami,

of chronic stomach pains, which he not illogically blamed on the ruling class. But was Zangara the real killer? Twenty-six years later—based on the death-bed testimony of another Chicago mobster, Roger Touhy—reporter Kenneth Allsop finally got to the bottom of the case:

"In the crowd near Zangara," Allsop wrote in his book *The Bootleggers*, "was another armed man—a Capone hired killer. In the flurry of shots six people were hit—but the bullet that struck Cermak was a .45 and not from the .32 calibre pistol used by Zangara. It was fired by the unknown Capone man who took advantage of the confusion to accomplish his mission."

Giuseppe Zangara, in short, was a diversion, a patsy. Even back then, the mob had shown the willingness, and the capacity, to dust a president just to whack a mayor. There is no way of knowing, however, if Jack Ruby had ever heard this story, when as a teenager he ran errands for Capone. Nevertheless, as David Scheim had reminded us in his book *Contract on America*, in the new world, just as in the old, shooting politicians, or throwing acid in the eyes of inquiring reporters, was a well-established family tradition.

Mayor Cermak was invited to the reviewing stand as the newly-elected president, Franklin Delano Roosevelt, prepared to address a local rally. Suddenly a man by the name of Giuseppe Zangara stepped from the crowd and fired five shots at the President. Zangara missed FDR, but a bullet hit and killed Mayor Cermak.

In the investigation which followed, it was determined that Zangara was a lone nut who suffered from "psychotic delusions." The gunman was apparently a victim

A Dead Man Turns Thirty

The State of the Case Today Controversy

I n the weeks after his selection of Senator Albert Gore to be his vice presidential running mate, then Governor Bill Clinton of Arkansas took a bus tour through the American midwest with his wife Hillary, and with Al and Tipper Gore. One evening along that road, Clinton was asked by a member of the accompanying press if he had an opinion concerning who killed John F. Kennedy. At the time, the film *JFK* had just been released on videocassette, and the controversy surrounding it was bubbling up again. Clinton smiled at the reporter and said "I think I'll let Senator Gore answer that question."

Gore responded that No, he did not believe that Lee Harvey Oswald, acting alone, was responsible for the murder of JFK; and that Yes, he did in fact believe that John Kennedy had been killed as a result of a conspiracy. But what did Bill Clinton think, the press persisted. "I

agree with Senator Gore," said the next President of the United States.

T HIRTY YEARS AFTER THE MURDER OF JOHN Kennedy, the overwhelming majority of American citizens—including, apparently, the current President, and Vice-President of the United States—have come to believe that the case against the men who killed the President is still open, and that at least some of the murderers had been allowed to skip free in the aftermath of the crime. Citing Cold War national security concerns as the barrier, the federal agencies involved, starting with the Warren Commission, had chosen not to probe into those areas where clues into the real murderers could possibly be found.

It had been a bit like pulling teeth, but thirty years after the murder of JFK it was now widely known that both the CIA and the FBI had withheld from the Warren commissioners, and indirectly, from the American public, vital information concerning the context of the case. Then, as now, the trail led back to Cuba, an aspect of the case on which both the FBI and the CIA had—until the time of the Church Committee hearings—remained vigilantly silent.

Today, save for a few remaining, incredibly powerful Warren Commission apologists, most serious students of the Kennedy murder have come to believe that the President was killed as the result of a conspiracy among angry Cuban exiles, certain furious mob bosses, and perhaps a few renegade CIA agents.

These insights, moreover, have been the result of one of the most fascinating and persistent political debates ever to take place in this country— the thirty year debate over who killed John F. Kennedy.

I T WOULD BE MISLEADING, OF COURSE, TO claim that the critics themselves have now reached a unanimity of opinion after thirty years of hammering away at this subject. Indeed, the critics themselves are still largely divided into two warring camps. One group of critics, led by Robert Blakey, is convinced that JFK's murder was a high-level mob operation, involving the Carlos Marcello crime family in New Orleans. Another group of critics, led by Anthony Summers and David Lifton, argues persuasively that the mob alone could never have opened all the doors necessary to allow a

public assassination of this nature to take place. These critics believe that at various critical junctures, the conspiracy had been nudged along through the tacit cooperation of at least a few key government officials. There remained a strong "hunch"—and let us not call it more than that—that the real culprits could, in the end, be found on the early 1960s payroll of the Central Intelligence Agency— or at the very least, on the payrolls of one of the Agency's numerous sister Intelligence organizations.

Based on the precedent established by the death of President Lincoln, this debate will undoubtedly continue for decades, if not for centuries, to come.

B Y 1993, WHAT remains most profoundly at issue is the will of the American people to get to the bottom of this case. As he left his chair at the House Select Committee in 1979, Robert Blakey turned over to incoming President Ronald Reagan's Justice Department a viable game plan for further investigation. Blakey recommended that, starting with the acoustical evidence, all of his Dealey Plaza testings be reexamined in detail. Critic Josiah Thompson suggested as well that a few additional scientific experiments be undertaken. "We have an acoustic fingerprint for Blakey's fourth shot," Thompson has commented. "I would sure like to know what might be obtained if we developed similiar fingerprints for the other three."

Blakey also recommended that Justice now take a fresh and uncensored look at all the links which had been developed between the Marcello mob family, and some of the crime's main principals, such as Oswald, Ruby, Banister and Ferrie. Recent revelations by mob lawyer Frank Ragano add an additional degree of urgency to this request. Presidents Reagan and Bush showed no inclination for this new investigation. What will be the fate of this request under our new President, Bill Clinton?

Finally, we have the unfinished business of all of those still secret files. Much has been made, by Oliver Stone and others, about the need to air those documents. The Cold War, after all, is now over. Still, the current plan to release these documents, after they have been screened by a select panel of four new Allen Dulleses, does not seem like a particularly promising approach. If the American public chooses to make enough noise about this matter, it still seems possible to obtain unedited copies of those files.

Thirty years on, it is clear that the bullets which killed John Kennedy also put an end to a state of innocence which once upon a time allowed us, in a manner of a covenant, to look upon our government, and our politicians, in a much more tranquil light. Since John Kennedy's death, we have all learned of the extremes to which our own secret warriors had often gone during the Cold War to protect this nation from the threat of diminished resources brought about by the claims of insurgent left-wing movements hostile to continued American control of those natural resources which exist within their own politically corrupted countries.

In fairness, it can be said that to protect us from this threat, these warriors were too often willing to risk the imposition of a right-wing, fascistic totalitarianism of their own making. In the minds of at least some of the foot soldiers in this drama, that "national security" effort included assassinating the President of the United States.

THE MURDER OF JOHN F. KENNEDY thus represented a lethal blow aimed at the heritage of democratic rule in America. Today, at the end of the Cold War, unless this entire national security establishment is purged of all such remaining covert elements, can anyone ensure we will not face more dark days on the road ahead?

We hope that President Clinton and Vice President Gore remember their words out on the campaign trail. Even the problems of deficit financing pale before the challenge of ensuring that our government remains a democracy in more than name only.

SOURCES

Chapter 1

As identified in the text, a verbatim transcript of District Attorney Henry Wade's press conference appeared in the *New York Times* on November 26, 1963. A biographical sketch of Wade was printed by the *Times* two days later, on November 28, 1963. For the details of the secret wartime collaboration between the Mafia and the U.S. Navy, see *The Luciano Project* by Rodney Campbell, published by McGraw-Hill in 1977. Campbell's account is based, in part, on the *Herland's Report*, the U.S. Navy's own reconstruction of this dark and pivotal period in recent U.S. history. For further information on the subject, see also the early chapters of *The Politics of Heroin in Southeast Asia* by Alfred W. McCoy, reprinted in a revised paperback edition by Harper & Row in 1991.

Chapter 2

Mark Lane has reprinted his original *National Guardian* response as an appendix to his most recent book on the Kennedy assassination, *Plausible Denial*, published by Thunder's Mouth Press in 1991. As noted in the sidebar to Chapter 36 of this book, Richard Condon would in time be drawn further into the Kennedy controversy. His own Kennedy assassination novel, *Winter Kills*, would be published by Dial Press in 1974. Under the direction of John Huston, the book would be made into a movie of the same name in 1979.

Chapter 3

Thomas J. Buchanan's *Who Killed Kennedy* was first published in the U.S. by Putnam in 1964. The next year Marzini and Martell published Joachim Joesten's *Oswald: Assassin or Fall Guy?* With an important section of the book first appearing in the March, 1964 edition of the magazine *Commentary*, Leo Sauvage's *The Oswald Affair: An Examination of the Contradictions and Omissions of the Warren Report* was published, in Cleveland, by the World Publishing Company in 1966.

Chapter 4

The "Revilo Oliver" controversy is discussed in some detail in the February 24, 1964, and the March 30, 1964, editions of *Newsweek*. See also the Peter Kihss article in the *New York Times*, February 10, 1964, pg 18. For a more sympathetic treatment of the professor, see the unsigned editorial opinion expressed in the April 7, 1964 edition of William Buckley's *National Review*. Morris Beale's snappy little novella, *Guns of the Regressive Right* was first published in Washington D.C., by the Columbia Publishing Company in 1964. The George Bush/Young Americans for Freedom anecdote is taken verbatim from a formerly secret Houston FBI headquarters report filed on November 23, 1963. The document was declassified and made available to the critics in the late 1970s, under the Freedom of Information Act.

Chapter 5

Murray Kempton's most comprehensive report of the Jack Ruby trial can be found in the March 7, 1964 edition of the *New Republic*. The offensive Tom Howard quote can be found in a subsequent Kempton book review of the Ruby trial, published in the November 25, 1965 edition of the same magazine. The George Bush/"Dusty" Miller anecdote is from an October 13, 1970 declassified White House memo from Charles W. Colson to H. R. Haldeman. The full memo is quoted, verbatim, as follows:

"October 13, 1970

MEMORANDUM FOR H.R. HALDEMAN

"Duster" Miller, who heads the Southern Region for the Teamsters, is actively backing George Bush with money and political support.

Charles W. Colson

cc: Harry Dent

George Bell—Be certain this guy is in our Labor book and rewarded appropriately."

Chapters 6-10

The Warren Commission's conclusions can be found in the first few chapters of *The Warren Commission Report* reprinted in a special facsimile edition by Marboro Books Corporation, a division of Barnes and Noble, in 1992. For the best in-depth analysis of this Report, see *Accessories After the Fact: The Warren Commission, the Authorities & the Report* by Sylvia Meagher, reprinted in 1992 by Vintage Books, a division of Random House. For the possibility that Oswald's intended target may have been John Connally, and not JFK, see Chapter 11 of James Reston Jr.'s *The Lone Star: The Live of John Connally* published in New York by Harper & Row in 1992.

Chapter 11

Bertrand Russell's comments appear, starting on page six, in the September 6, 1964 issue of *A Minority of One.* I.F. Stone's response may be found in the October 5, 1964 issue of *I.F. Stone's Weekly.*

Chapter 12

Dr. Renatus Hartog's *The Two Assassins*, written with Lucy Freeman, was first published by the T. Cromwell Company in New York in 1965. Kerry Thornley's *Oswald* was published the same year, in Chicago, by New Classics House, a division of Novel Books, Inc. *Portrait of the Assassin* by Gerald R. Ford and John R. Stiles was also published in 1965, by Simon & Schuster. Upon its declassification, the full transcript of "The Waggoner Conference" was published, with analysis, in 1974, by Harold Weisberg, as *Whitewash IV: JFK Assassination Transcript*, in Weisberg's ongoing, self-published, *Whitewash* series. George Lardner's article about Gerald Ford's connection to the FBI can be found on page A10 in the Friday, January 20, 1978, issue of *The Washington Post.*

Chapter 13

Edward J. Epstein's *Inquest: The Warren Commission and the Establishment of Truth* was published in New York by the Viking Press in 1966. Mark Lane's *Rush to Judgment: A Critique of the Warren Commission's Inquiry into the Murder of President John F. Kennedy, Officer J.D. Tippit, and Lee Harvey Oswald* was published, in New York, by Holt, Rinehart and Winston later in the same year. The O'Neill-Sibert FBI Autopsy Report was reprinted in 1966 in Richard K. Popkin's *The Second Oswald*, published jointly, in New York, by the New York Review of Books and Avon Books.

Chapter 14

For Allen Dulles's record at the CIA, see *The Invisible Government* by David Wise and Thomas B. Ross, published by Vintage Books, a division of Random House, in New York, in February, 1974. For more on John McCloy, see *The Wise Men: Six Friends And The World They Made* by Walter Isaacson & Evan Thomas, published in 1986 by Touchstone, a division of Simon & Schuster.

Chapter 15

One can get a good sense of the integrity of men like Sam Holland and Lee Bowers in the Mark Lane and Emile de Antonio documentary, *The Plot to Kill JFK: Rush to Judgment*, released by MPI Home Video in 1988.

Chapter 16

Vincent Salandria's important early articles on Dealey Plaza have never been collected in book form. See the January and March 1965 issues of *Liberation* for two of the best. Revised and updated, Harold Weisberg's *Whitewash* book series is now available, in a single volume, from Carroll & Graff. For George C. Thomson's musings, see *The Quest for Truth: (A Quizzical Look at the Warren Report), or How President Kennedy Really Was Assassinated*, privately printed by The G. C. Engineering Company, in Glendale, California, in 1964. For an update on Thomson's views, see "The Kennedy Hoax [That Tippit Impersonated JFK in the Car] as published in the October 13, 1968 edition of the *National Insider.*

Chapter 17

The CIA Book Critic's memo is reprinted as an appendix to *Destiny Betrayed: The Kennedy Assassination and the Garrison Trial* by James DiEugenio, published in New York by the Sheridan Square Press in 1992. *Nomenclature of an Assassination Cabal* is included in *The JFK Reader* published by Prevailing Wings Research, in Santa Barbara, in 1972. As edited by self-declared CIA agent Paul Renzo, *Beyond the Gemstone File* was once announced as available from Fighting Tigers Publications, in South Lake Tahoe, California, back in 1980. Xerox copies of sections of the manuscript have circulated widely among buffs over the years. The manuscript is, of course, an educated schoolboy hoax.

Chapter 18

The Scavengers and Critics of the Warren Report by Richard Warren Lewis, based on an investigation by Lawrence Schiller, was published by Dell Paperbacks in New York in 1967. *The Truth About the Assassination* by Charles Roberts was published in New York by Grosset & Dunlap the same year. Based on the television "CBS News Inquiry: The Warren Report," *Should We Now Believe the Warren Report?* by Stephen White was published in New York by MacMillan in 1968. The annual CIA/CBS New Year's Day Party is described in some detail in Chapter 27 of *Dulles: A Biography of Eleanor, Allen and John Foster Dulles and their Family Network*, by Leonard Mosely, published in New York by the Dial Press/James Wade in 1978. For additional information on the unique CIA/CBS relationship, see also "The CIA and The Media" by Carl Bernstein in the October 10, 1977 issue of *Rolling Stone*. Dan Rather's recollections of viewing the Zapruder film are included in his 1977 autobiography *The Camera Never Blinks, Adventures of a TV Journalist*, published in New York by William Morrow and Company.

Chapter 19

For Sylvia Meagher's full accounting of "The Odio Incident," see "The Proof of the Plot" section of Chapter 21 of *Accessories After the Fact*, reissued in 1992 in paperback by Vintage Books, a division of Random House. For a summary of the "Three Tramps Controversy," see "The Kennedy Assassination's Links To the Here and Now" by Edgar F. Tatro in 1990 in the ongoing, JFK assassination magazine, *The Third Decade*.

Chapter 20

For the Cuba Connection, see *Deadly Secrets: The CIA-Mafia War Against Castro and The Assassination of JFK* by Warren Hinckle and William Turner, published in New York by Thunder's Mouth Press in 1992. The activities of Alpha 66 in Texas are charted in "Dallas: The Cuban Connection" by George O'Toole and Paul Hoch, which first appeared in the March 1976 issue of *The Saturday Evening Post*, and "Dallas Mosaic: The Cops, the Cubans and the Company" by Philip Melanson, in *The Third Decade*, Vol. 1, #3, March, 1985. For a full accounting of "The Anthony Veciana/Maurice Bishop Controversy," see *The Last Investigation* by Gaeton Fonzi published in New York by Thunder's Mouth Press in 1993.

Chapters 21 & 22

Josiah Thompson's *Six Seconds in Dallas: A Micro-Study of the Kennedy Assassination* was first published by Bernard Geis Associates, in association with Random House, in 1967. Out of print for many years, a revised and updated edition of this important book is long overdue. "The Case for Three Assassins," by David Welsh and David Lifton, was first published in the January 1967 edition of *Ramparts*.

Chapter 23

The best early writing on the "Camp Street Cabal" can be found in *Oswald in New Orleans* by Harold Weisberg, published in paperback, in New York, by Canyon Books in 1967. See also *The Plot to Kill The President* by G. Robert Blakey and Richard N.Billings, published by Times Books, a division of Quadrangle/New York Times Books, in 1981.

Chapter 24

For a critical look at Jim Garrison, and the Clay Shaw trial, see *American Grotesque: An Account of the Clay Shaw-Jim Garrison Affair in the City of New Orleans* by James Kirkwood, published by Simon & Schuster in New York in 1968. For a local perspective, see also *Plot or Politics: The Garrison Case & Its Cast* by Rosemary James and Jack Wardlaw, published by the Pelican Publishing House in New Orleans in 1967. The homosexual dimension to the Shaw Trial is discussed in Chapter 8 of *Scandals, Scamps and Scoundrels: The Casebook of an Investigative Reporter* by James Phelan, published in New York by Random House in 1992.

Chapter 25

Jack Anderson's Johnny Roselli columns were syndicated from January through April of 1971. The official story was ultimately revealed in *Alleged Assassination Plots Involving Foreign Leaders, An Interim Report of the Select Committee to Study Governmental Operations with Regard to Intelligence Activities*, published by the U.S. Government Printing Office on November 20, 1975. The full *Church Committee Report* starts here, and runs over the course of five subsequently issued volumes. Richard Nixon's associations with the Batista regime are reported in "Nixon and the Mafia" by Jeff Gerth, *Sundance* magazine, November/December, 1972. See also *All-American Mafioso: The Johnny Roselli Story* by Charles Rappleye and Ed Becker, published by Doubleday in New York in September, 1991.

Chapter 26

For Richard Nixon's Bay of Pigs conversation with H. R. Haldeman, see "From Dallas to Watergate" by Jonathan Marshall, *West, The Magazine of the San Jose Mercury*, for November 20, 1983. The Edward Lansdale "Immaculate Deception" incident is from *Deadly Secrets* by Warren Hinckle and William Turner. See Chapter 20, above, for full citation.

Chapter 27

For Lee Harvey Oswald and the Lone Avenger theory, see *The Assassination of John F. Kennedy: The Reasons Why* by Albert H. Newman, published in New York by Clarkson N. Potter, Inc. in 1970; *Clearing The Air* by Daniel Schorr, published in Boston by The Houghton Mifflin Company in 1977; and *Oswald's Game* by Jean Davison, published in New York by W.W. Norton & Company in 1983. For Oswald as a possible KGB operative, see *Legend: The Secret World of Lee Harvey Oswald* by Edward Jay Epstein, published in New York by The Viking Press in 1979, and *The Oswald File* by Michael Eddowes, published in New York by Clarkson N. Potter in 1977. For Oswald's early life in New Orleans, see *The Plot to Kill the President* by G. Robert Blakey and Richard N. Billings, as cited in Chapter 23, above. For Oswald's Marine career and life in the Soviet Union, see *Legend: The Secret World of Lee Harvey Oswald* by Edward Jay Epstein, cited above. For Oswald's relations with the White Russian Community, see *The Dallas Connection* by Peter Dale Scott, an unpublished manuscript available in xerox, with the author's permission, from Tom Davis Books in Santa Cruz, California. For Oswald and the CIA, see *Spy Saga: Lee Harvey Oswald and U.S. Intelligence* by Philip H. Melanson, published in New York by Praeger in 1990. For Oswald's Cuba politics, see *Conspiracy* by Anthony Summers, reissued in a revised, updated edition by Paragon House in New York, 1992. For Oswald's possible visits to the moon, see "Did Lee Harvey Oswald Drop Acid?" by Marin A. Lee, Robert Ranftel, and Jeff Cohen, *Rolling Stone*, March 3, 1983.

Chapter 28

Seth Kantor's *The Ruby Cover-Up* was first published in New York by Zebra Books, a division of the Kensington Publishing Company, in 1978. For another side of Jack Ruby, see *Jack Ruby's Girls* by Diana Hunter and Alice Anderson, A Genesis Press Book, published by Hallux, Inc. in Atlanta in 1970. For the "Disappearing Witnesses" controversy, see the four-volume *Forgive My Grief* series by Penn Jones, Jr., published by the Midlothian Mirror Press in Midlothian, Texas, beginning in 1966.

Chapter 29

The history of the House Select Committee on Assassinations is chronicled in two invaluable newsletters: *Echoes of Conspiracy* (EOC) edited and published by Paul Hoch in Berkeley, California; and *Clandestine America*, the Washington Newsletter of the Assassinations Information Bureau.

Chapter 30

For a good summary of "Blakey's problem," see *The Plot to Kill the President* by G. Robert Blakey and Richard N. Billings, as cited in the notes for Chapter 23. For the "Umbrella Man" controversy, see *The Flight of CE-399: Evidence of Conspiracy* by Robert B. Cutler, self-published in Beverly, Massachusetts by Cutler Designs in 1970.

Chapter 31

For more on Jack Ruby and the Dallas police, see *Conspiracy* by Anthony Summers, as cited in the notes for Chapter 27. See also *The Ruby Cover-Up* by Seth Kantor, as cited in the notes for Chapter 28, and "Dallas Mosaic: The Cops, The Cubans and The Company" by Philip Melanson, *The Third Decade*, Vol. #1, #3, March 1985.

Chapter 32

For the relationship between Lucky Luciano and the U.S. Navy, see *The Luciano Project* by Rodney Campbell, published in New York by McGraw-Hill in 1977. For the continuing role of the CIA in the international drug trade, see both *The Politics of Heorin in Southeast Asia* by Alfred E. McCoy, revised and republished in New York by Harper & Row in paperback in 1990; and *Drug Wars: Corrupton, Counterinsurgency and Covert Operations in the Third World* by Jonathan Marshall, published by Cohan & Cohen in Forestville, California in 1991. For background information on the World Anti-Communist League, see *Inside The League: The Shocking Expose of How Terrorists, Nazis, and Latin American Death Squads Have Infiltrated the World Anti-Communist League* by Scott and Jon Lee Anderson, published in New York by the Dodd, Mead Company in 1986.

Chapter 33

Now in its thirteenth printing, *Best Evidence: Disguise and Deception in the Assassination of John F. Kennedy* by David S. Lifton, is published in New York by Carroll & Graf Publishers, Inc.

Chapter 34

Charles A. Crenshaw's *JFK: Conspiracy of Silence* , written with Jens Hansen and J. Gary Shaw, was first published by Signet, a division of The Penguin Group, in New York in April, 1992. *High Treason* by Robert J. Groden and Harrison Edward Livingstone, was first published in paperback by the Berkley Publishing Group in November, 1990.

Chapter 35

For much more on the mob connection, see *Mafia Kingfish: Carlos Marcello and the Assassination of John F. Kennedy* by John H. Davis, published in New York by Signet/New American Library, a division of the Penguin Group, in 1989. See also *Contract On America: The Mafia Murder of President John F. Kennedy* by David E. Scheim, published in New York by Zebra Paperbacks, a division of the Kensington Publishing Group, in 1988. For Frank Ragano's story, see "'I Want Kennedy Killed!' Hoffa Shouted: An Eyewitness Account" by Jack Newfield, *Penthouse*, January 1992.

Chapter 36

My Story by Judith Exner, as told to Ovid Demaris, was first published by Grove Press in New York, 1977. For an update, see the three-part series "JFK, the Mob, & Me" by Judith Exner, as told to Anthony Summers, which appeared in the *New York Daily News*, October 6-8, 1991. Richard Condon's *The Manchurian Candidate* was first published by McGraw Hill, in New York, in 1959. The author's later "Kennedy" novel, *Winter Kills*, was published in New York by the Dial Press in 1974. Vance Bourjaily's *The Man Who Knew Kennedy* was also published by the Dial Press in 1967. Harry J. Jones' *A Private Army* was first published in New York by Collier Books in 1969. A revised edition, with a new title, *The Minuteman*, was published by Doubleday in 1968. Barry N. Malzberg's *The Destruction of the Temple* was first published in New York by Pocket Books in 1974. Wesley S. Thurston's *The Trumpets of November* was first published by Bernard Geis in 1966. J. G. Ballard's most important Kennedy essays can be found in *The Atrocity Exhibition* published in San Francisco by Re/Search Editions in 1990. For the impact of the Kennedy assassination on the Punk Generation, see *Dead Kennedys: The Unauthorized Version* by f-Stop Fitzgerald published in San Francisco by Last Gasp Books & Comics in 1983. *Assassination Rhapsody* by Derek Pell was published in Brooklyn by Semiotext(e) in 1989. Finally, Don DeLillo's *Libra* was first published in paperback by Penguin/NAL in 1989.

Chapter 37

For the Oliver Stone controversy, see *JFK: The Book Of The Film* by Oliver Stone and Zachary Sklar, published in New York by Applause Books in 1992. Jim Garrison's *On The Trail of the Assassins* was first published in paperback by Warner Books, in New York, in 1991. John M. Newman's *JFK and Vietnam* was also published by Warner Brothers, in hardcover, in 1992.

Chapter 38

President Clinton and Vice President Gore's remarks on the JFK Assassination were reported, over the wire, by the Associated Press in July, 1992.

A Note on How to Obtain Source Materials

Many of the titles reviewed in this Handbook are still in print, and can be found in bookstores across the country. For the harder-to-find titles, write to **Tom Davis Books, P.O. Box 1107, Aptos CA 95001**; **The Last Hurrah Bookshop, 937 Memorial Avenue, Williamsport PA 17701**; and/or **The President's Box Bookshop, P.O. Box 1255, Washington DC 20013**. For individual articles, contact the **Assassination Archives and Research Center, 98 F Street N.W., Suite 510, Washington DC 20004**. The telephone number is (202) 393-1917. Thanks to the owners and/or staffs of each of these concerns for helping provide materials for *Who Shot JFK?*

Bob Callahan is the author of *Who Shot JFK?* A former speech writer for Senator Robert F. Kennedy, Callahan is a 1978 recipient of a Writer's Fellowship from the National Endowment for the Arts. From his San Francisco-based studio he is currently creating, in association with Art Spiegelman, a series of illustrated crime thrillers for Avon Paperbacks, called NEON LIT: NOIR ILLUSTRATED. Mr. Callahan claims that he can vividly recall exactly where he was standing on August 6, 1976, the moment he learned that gangster Johnny Roselli had washed ashore in an oil drum off Miami Beach.

E.J. Muller, who lives and works in Alameda, California, designed *Who Shot JFK?* on a Macintosh IIsi computer, using QuarkXpress software. He also served as line editor and art director for this book. An accomplished sports and business journalist, Mr. Muller is also curator of the San Francisco Historical Boxing Museum. He is currently working on a book about boxing culture at the turn of the century, being produced at the Bob Callahan Studios. Mr. Muller had just graduated from high school, and was preparing to enter the San Francisco Art Institute, when he learned of Johnny Roselli's untimely demise.

One of America's reigning masters of *noir* graphics, **Mark Zingarelli** has had work published in *Esquire, The New Yorker, Entertainment Weekly* and the *Village Voice. Real Life*, a collection of his own true crime short stories, is available from Fantagraphic Books in Seattle. From his home in rural Stanwood, Washington, Zingarelli is currently adapting William Lindsay Gresham's classic carnival novel, *Nightmare Alley*, for the forthcoming NEON LIT series. Mr. Zingarelli was unaware, until mid-way through this project, that Mr. Roselli had been sealed in an oil drum and set adrift off the Florida coast.